HIGHWAY TO HEAVEN SERIES

Edward A. Fitzpatrick, *Editor*

Institute of Catechetical Research, Marquette University

THE VINE AND THE BRANCHES

BOOK OF THE HOLY CHILD (Grade One)

LIFE OF MY SAVIOR (Grade Two)

LIFE OF THE SOUL (Grade Three)

BEFORE CHRIST CAME (Grade Four)

THE VINE AND THE BRANCHES (Grade Five)

THE MISSAL (Grade Six)

HIGHWAY TO GOD (Grades Seven and Eight)

Accompanying this Series is the RELIGION IN LIFE CURRICULUM for grades one to six and PRACTICAL PROBLEMS IN RELIGION for grades seven and eight.

The Vine
and
The Branches

BY A SCHOOL SISTER OF NOTRE DAME
of the faculty of St. Paul Diocesan Teachers College,
St. Paul, Minn.

and

REV. R. G. BANDAS, Ph.D.Agg., S.T.D. et M.

*Professor of Dogmatic Theology and Catechetics, St. Paul
Seminary, Archdiocesan Director of the Confraternity
of Christian Doctrine, St. Paul, Minn.*

ST. AUGUSTINE ACADEMY PRESS
HOMER GLEN, ILLINOIS

Nihil obstat:
    GEORGE J. ZISKOVSKY,
        Censor deputatus

Jmprimatur:
    ✠ JOHN G. MURRAY,
        Archbishop of St. Paul

March 15, 1934

This book was originally published in 1934 by The Bruce Publishing Company.
This edition reprinted in 2017 by St. Augustine Academy Press
based on the 1935 second printing.
Some of the illustrations were replaced due to deterioration of the originals.

Softcover ISBN: 978-1-64051-034-0
Hardcover ISBN: 978-1-64051-035-7

My dear young readers:

This book tells you in a remarkable way about the history of our Church on earth. As the word is used in this book, it does not mean the church buildings, but the members who attend it. It includes all the faithful everywhere. Who are they? They are those who have been baptized. They believe the same doctrines as are contained in the Apostles' Creed. They are governed in this organization by the successors of the Apostles under one visible head on earth, the Pope. This congregation of all the faithful is the Roman Catholic Church — our Church — instituted by Christ Himself.

The great Church of Christ has existed for centuries since that first Pentecost Day when Christ sent the Holy Ghost to begin the Church. We come into contact with the Church of Christ through our own parish church. It is in our neighborhood. In it Christ is always ready to receive us in the Blessed Sacrament. To it we go to Mass every Sunday and on holydays of obligation. In it also we receive Holy Communion. And at other times, too, we go in reverently, kneel in a pew, take a seat, and pray to God.

If we study the history of the Church from the time of Christ, as we do in this book, we understand better what a great thing the parish church is. We understand better why we should visit it frequently, and why we should support it.

When we talk about the Church as we do in this book, we mean especially the *members* of the Church rather than the building. It includes all the members of the churches in all the world. We call it on earth a visible society or organization. This is the second meaning of the word "Church." Its first meaning is in the sense of a church building. It has a third and wider meaning. It includes all the saints in heaven, as well as all the faithful on earth. It includes, too, those persons who still suffer for their sins in purgatory. It is a great and glorious company. It goes back more than nineteen hundred years to Christ. It includes also all those whom Christ released from Limbo. It was established by Christ Himself. The Holy Ghost is always with it, and in it, as Christ promised. It is your high privilege to belong to it. You and your classmates, your parents, your friends, the priests and bishops, and the Pope are part of it, too. Christ is the Vine; all the rest are the branches.

Great and wonderful men and women have been a part of it in all times since Christ came to earth to redeem men. Think of the great procession since that day. Imagine passing before you, as they do in this book, Apostles like Peter and Paul and John, martyrs like St. Stephen and the Jesuit Martyrs of North America, founders of monasteries like St. Benedict, founders of religious orders like St. Francis, St. Dominic, St. Ignatius and others, world-wandering missionaries like St. Paul and St. Francis Xavier, great popes like Gregory VII and Innocent III and Leo XIII, great women like St. Monica, St. Teresa, and the Little Flower, and laymen like Frederick Ozanam, Thomas More, and Daniel O'Connell. And imagine, too, such great lovers of God and of men as St. John Baptist de la Salle, St. Vincent De Paul, St. Peter Fourier, and a thousand others.

The stories of these great saints and leaders of the Church are told for your benefit. You belong with them in the Church. They will pray for you. Honor them, and thank God that such heroic men and women are with you a member of the Communion of Saints. You and they are parts of the Mystical Body of Christ.

To help you appreciate the greatness of the Church and what your membership in it means, the authors of this book have added to their interesting biographies, some things especially for you to do. To make sure you have read the stories carefully, they ask you some questions about it under the heading: *"Can you answer these questions?"* If you cannot answer the questions, or are doubtful, read the story again to be sure about your answers. Look over your back lessons every once in a while. Learn by heart the quotations from Scripture that are given. If the book asks you to learn one, learn another one just for good measure. Look up in your Bible just where the passage came from and have teacher or mother tell you the whole story. You are given the opportunity of "something to do"; do it.

These will help you the better to understand the Church and the kind of life you must lead to be a worthy child of the Church of Christ.

All of us every day have little problems, just as the great saints had problems. Some of the problems which children in other schools have had are given in this book. Show by your answers that you know what is good and right. If such problems come into your life, remember the saints, and remember what you said you would do.

And in conclusion, remember you are a branch, and that Christ is the Vine, always sending into you the life of grace, if you are ready to receive it. The Vine is your support. It is your strength. It will be with you always. Love Christ who is the Vine.

EDWARD A. FITZPATRICK

The Catechetical Institute,
Marquette University.

CONTENTS

UNIT I

How the Church Had Its Beginning

Jesus came down from heaven to save us and show us the way to God. But He did not wish to remain on earth for all time. Therefore He gave us His Church, to teach the way to heaven in His place. The Church is like a great ship. All who are in it and remain faithful to the end, will reach the shores of heaven in safety. St. Peter, or his successor, the pope, is the Pilot who steers the ship. Jesus watches over it day and night to keep it on the right path.

The first three lessons in this book tell us how the Church had its beginning on earth and how God helped the Apostles in a wonderful way to convert the people and make them true Christians.

1

Upon the Blessed Virgin and the Apostles came
the Holy Ghost in flames like tongues of fire.

1. I Am the Vine

While Jesus was on earth, the people loved to sit around Him and listen to His wonderful stories. The stories that He told always had some hidden meaning and were intended to teach them about God and the kingdom of heaven.

One day Jesus said to those around Him: "I am the Vine, you are the branches." What did He mean? Have you ever seen a great grape vine winding its many branches in all directions? No matter where you found big clusters of grapes hidden under deep green leaves, you were always sure to see them growing on a branch, and that branch growing from another branch, and so on. At last you found, if you took the trouble to look, that all the branches came from one strong vine or stem that had its root hidden way down deep in the ground. All the fruit and branches really received their food and strength from the one big vine.

Jesus calls Himself the Vine. Can you see why? He did not wish to remain on earth forever, but He promised that, even if He did go back to heaven, He would still be with His people and be their life and strength, just as the vine is the life and strength of the branches and fruit.

"Behold, I am with you all days," said Jesus to His

Apostles, "even to the end of the world." Because He did not wish to remain on earth, He founded His Church and gave St. Peter and the other Apostles charge of it. He still guides His Church from within; He is the invisible leader. But He has also given us a visible leader; that is, the pope, the successor of St. Peter, who takes charge of the Church in His name.

The saints in heaven, the faithful on earth, and the souls in purgatory, all belong together; they are all the branches and fruit, and Christ is the Vine.

It is a glorious thing to belong to the Church of Christ! We should all be very happy to be branches of the true Vine, Jesus, the Son of God, who came to earth to save us.

Now answer these questions:

1. What did the stories teach which Jesus told?
2. How do the fruit and the branches of a vine receive their food?
3. What does Jesus call Himself?
4. Who is the invisible leader of the Church?
5. Who is the visible leader of the Church?
6. Who are the branches and the fruit that belong to Jesus, the Vine?

When we speak of the Church which Christ founded, we do not mean a building. We mean all those who are baptized, who believe in the teachings of Jesus Christ, and who are ruled by those who take the place of Christ on earth; that is, the pope, the bishops, and priests.

The blessed in heaven are the Church Triumphant.

The faithful on earth are the Church Militant.

The souls in purgatory are the Church Suffering.

All three together are called the Communion of Saints.

The Church teaches us the way to heaven, but we do not have to travel the way alone.

The Church Triumphant prays for us at the throne of God.

The members of the Church Militant walk side by side with us.

The Church Suffering looks to us for help and prays for us in return. What a glorious company to belong to. Did you ever stop to think that you are a member of the Communion of Saints?

Ask yourself:

Am I proud to belong to the Catholic Church?

Do I often call on the saints to help me?

Do I think of heaven as my true home?

Do I remember that others are traveling the same road to heaven with me?

Do I remember that I might be able to help others on the road to heaven, by keeping them from committing sin?

Do I pray for the suffering souls in purgatory?

Things to do:

1. Draw a grape vine with many branches. Under it write Christ's words: "I am the Vine, you are the branches."

2. Find a picture which shows Jesus telling the people stories.

3. Can you remember any of the stories Jesus told? Tell one of them to the class.

4. Draw a road going up a mountain. At the top make a cross to show heaven. Above it write the words: "Church

Triumphant." On the road show people traveling on the way to heaven. Near them write: "Church Militant." On the side of the hill draw a cave for purgatory and mark it "Church Suffering."

5. If you have a Missal, find the prayers which are said for the Church and the faithful before Consecration, and the others that follow Consecration. When you say these prayers at Mass, along with the priest, try to remember that you are part of that company. The prayers that the Church uses are the best for us all to use.

6. Read or sing Cardinal Newman's song, "Lead, Kindly Light." It will help you to remember that you are a pilgrim on the road to heaven.

7. Memorize one or more of the following Scripture texts and tell how they fit into this lesson:

"He that eateth My flesh, and drinketh My blood, abideth in Me, and I in him" (John vi. 57).

"As the living Father hath sent Me, and I live by the Father; so he that eateth Me, the same also shall live by Me."

Can you answer these questions?

1. Why did God create us?
2. What must we do to get to heaven?
3. How does God let us know what He wants us to believe?
4. Who founded the Church?
5. What is the Church?
6. Why did Christ found the Church?
7. Did Jesus found the Church for everybody or for just a few people?
8. Do all people belong to the Church?
9. What do you mean by the Communion of Saints?
10. How does the Church Triumphant help us?
11. How should we help the members of the Church Militant?

12. How should we help the Church Suffering?
13. When do we celebrate the Feast of All Saints?
14. When do we celebrate the Feast of All Souls?
15. Who are the souls in purgatory?
16. How can you gain an indulgence?
17. What is an indulgence?

Good things to read:

"Abou Ben Adhem," *American Reader V*, page 308.
"A Tale of All Soul's Eve," *Rosary Reader V*, page 89.
"The First Miracle of Jesus," *De La Salle Reader V*, page 42.
"God Is Our Father," *De La Salle Reader V*, page 154.
"The Lord's Prayer," *Rosary Reader V*, page 60.

2. Peter, the First Pope

It was early morning on the Sea of Galilee. The Apostles were coming back with boats empty. They had fished all night and had caught nothing. On the seashore in the misty distance stood a lone figure, watching them come in. Who could it be, they wondered?

"Have you anything to eat?" called the Stranger to them.

"Nothing!"

"Throw out your nets to the right," He told them.

To the right! that was no place to fish; but something made them obey. Soon their nets were so full that they could hardly drag them in.

John, one of the Apostles, looked up. He knew that

there was only one person in the world who saw all things and could do all things.

"It is the Lord," he said to Peter.

Peter did not wait to hear more. It was Jesus, and Peter loved Him above everything else. He jumped into the water and swam ashore. The others followed quickly. They were always happy when they could be with Jesus.

Near the shore Jesus had a fire and some food ready, for He knew they must be very hungry after a night out at sea. He was always having happy little surprises like that for them.

They sat down to eat. After the meal Jesus said to Simon Peter:

"Simon, lovest thou Me more than these?"

Peter answered: "Yea, Lord, Thou knowest that I love Thee."

Jesus said: "Feed My lambs."

A second time Jesus asked: "Simon, lovest thou Me?"

And Peter again answered: "Yea, Lord, Thou knowest that I love Thee."

Jesus said: "Feed My lambs."

Then He asked a third time: "Lovest thou Me?"

Peter became sad. Was Jesus thinking of the time, not long past, when Peter had denied Him three times? He answered with all his heart: "Lord, Thou knowest all things: Thou knowest that I love Thee."

"Feed My sheep," Jesus said to him.

With these words Jesus meant to tell Peter that he was to rule over the lambs and sheep of His flock; that

"And I will give to thee the keys
of the kingdom of heaven."

is, over the people and also over the priests and bishops belonging to the Church.

Once before, when Peter and Jesus had met, Jesus had made this promise to him: "Thou art Peter (rock) and on this rock I will build My Church, and the gates of hell shall not prevail against it, and I will give to thee the keys of the kingdom of heaven. And whatsoever thou shalt bind upon earth, it shall be bound also in heaven: and whatsoever thou shalt loose on earth, it shall be loosed also in heaven" (Matt. xvi. 15–19).

And now Jesus kept His promise. Peter was made the head of the Church on earth. We shall see later how he watched over the lambs and sheep of his flock and how his flock looked up to him as their leader. They knew Jesus wanted it so.

Now answer these questions:
1. What were the Apostles doing on the sea of Galilee?
2. Who was the Stranger on the shore?
3. What did He ask them?
4. What did He tell them to do?
5. Who first knew that it was Jesus on the shore?
6. Why did Peter jump into the water and swim to shore?
7. What did Jesus have ready for the Apostles on the shore?
8. What did Jesus ask Peter after the meal?
9. Why was Peter sad?
10. What did Jesus mean to tell Peter?
11. Who is meant by the lambs and the sheep?
12. Why did everybody look upon Peter as the leader?

———————

Jesus chose Peter to take His place on earth. When Peter died, another person took his place as head of the Church, and so it went on to the present day. In all, there have been 261 popes, including Pope Pius XI.

Like St. Peter, the pope of today takes the place of Christ on earth. He is the visible head of the Church. He feeds the lambs and the sheep of his flock. Every faithful little lamb should love him and think of him very often. Perhaps some day you will be able to travel to Rome to see the pope and receive his blessing. What a happy day that will be.

The pope is called the Holy Father. He lives in a large palace called the Vatican. There are many interesting things to be found in the Vatican. Perhaps you would like to read more about it.

The following prayer for the pope is used by the priest at Mass. Read it carefully and say it often:

Prayer for the Pope

O God, the shepherd and ruler of all the faithful, look down favorably upon Thy servant N., whom Thou hast been pleased to appoint pastor over Thy Church; grant, we beseech Thee, that he may serve by word and example those over whom he is set, and so attain to eternal life with the flock committed to his care. Through our Lord Jesus Christ, Thy Son, who liveth and reigneth with Thee, in the unity of the Holy Ghost, God, world without end. Amen.

Things to do:

1. Find the story of the meeting between Jesus and Peter and tell it to the class.

2. Look for a picture or statue of St. Peter and see what he holds in his hand.

3. Draw the keys of Peter and write the words of Jesus to Peter under them.

4. On the map find the sea of Galilee.

5. Draw or cut out a picture of the sea of Galilee with the Apostles' boat on it. Write the story in your own words.

6. A shepherd usually carries a staff. A bishop also has a staff. Find what the bishop's staff is called.

7. Who is at the head of the Church today, in place of St. Peter, the first pope?

8. Learn the "Hymn for the Pope."

9. Find pictures and newspaper and magazine articles about the pope and tell the class what you have read.

10. If you have read something about the Vatican, tell the class about it.

11. Memorize the Scripture text in this lesson.

Can you answer these questions?

1. Why could Jesus see and know all things?

2. Who is the invisible head of the Church?

3. Who is the visible head of the Church?

4. Who are the lambs and the sheep of the flock?

5. What did Jesus mean when He said: "And whatsoever thou shalt bind upon earth, it shall be bound also in heaven: and whatsoever thou shalt loose on earth, it shall be loosed also in heaven"? (Matt. xvi. 19.)

6. Can the enemies of the Church ever destroy her? What words of Jesus tell us that they cannot?

Good things to read:

"Four Fishermen," *Catholic Youth Reader V*, page 70.

"Quo Vadis," *Shield's Reader V*, page 191.

"Peter is Given the Keys of the Kingdom of Heaven," *Bible History*, Sister Anna Louise.

"The Rock of St. Peter," *De La Salle Reader VI*.

"The Rock of St. Peter," *Catholic National Reader VI*.

Hymn for the Pope

Long live the Pope!
His praises sound
Again and yet again:
His rule is over space and time;
His throne the hearts of men:
All hail! the Shepherd King of Rome,
The theme of loving song:
Let all the earth his glory sing,
And heav'n the strain prolong.
Let all the earth his glory sing,
And heav'n the strain prolong.

Beleaguered by the foes of earth,
Beset by hosts of hell,
He guards the loyal flock of Christ,
A watchful sentinel:
And yet, amid the din and strife,
The clash of mace and sword,
He bears alone the shepherd staff,
This champion of the Lord.
He bears alone the shepherd staff,
This champion of the Lord.

Then raise the chant, with heart and voice,
In church and school and home:
"Long live the Shepherd of the Flock!
Long live the Pope of Rome!"
Almighty Father, bless his work,
Protect him in his ways,
Receive his pray'rs, fulfill his hopes,
And grant him "length of days!"
Receive his pray'rs, fulfill his hopes,
And grant him "length of days!"

3. The Birthday of the Church

Everything was very quiet in the Upper Room at Jerusalem. For nine days the Blessed Mother and the Apostles had been staying together with other friends of Jesus, watching and praying. Jesus had ascended into heaven. How lonely they must have been without Him! But He had told them to watch and pray until He would send them the Holy Ghost. And so they prayed and waited.

All at once there was a rushing sound, as if a strong wind were whirling through the air. Then softly, gently, came flames like tongues of fire from above, and rested over the heads of those who were gathered in the Upper Room. Jesus had kept His promise. The Holy Ghost had come.

"Did you hear that noise?" asked the people in the city. "What do you suppose it is?" And they ran to the house from which the rushing sound seemed to come.

Ever since Jesus had been crucified, the Apostles were afraid to show themselves, for fear that they, too, would be killed. But now that the Holy Ghost was with them, everything was different. Now they had courage to face the whole world. The doors of the Upper Room were unlocked and the Apostles went out to speak to the people. And as they spoke, a strange thing happened. The many visitors who were at Jerusalem at this time, spoke different languages. There were people from Arabia and Asia, from Egypt and Rome. And yet, no one had to ask what the Apostles were saying. Each one understood the words of the Apostles, for "every man heard them speak in his own tongue." That was the work of the Holy Ghost. He gave to the Apostles the gift of tongues and to the people who listened the grace to understand.

But as always, when someone tries to do good, there were men who laughed at the Apostles. They said that the Apostles were drunk and did not know what they were talking about. Then Peter raised his hand and began to speak:

"Men of Judea," he said, "these men are not drunk, as you say; for it is still early in the day. But the Lord has poured His spirit over them, as He promised the prophet Joel many years ago. And now listen to my words: Jesus of Nazareth, whom you crucified, rose again from the dead. We ourselves saw Him go to heaven. Today He sent down the Holy Ghost upon us. He will also send His spirit over you, if you will turn to Him and believe in Him."

Many Jews were deeply touched by the words of Peter. "What shall we do?" they asked.

"Do penance and be baptized," answered the Apostle. And 3,000 persons were baptized that same day.

That visit of the Holy Ghost was the beginning of the Church or the birthday of the Church. It is called the Feast of Pentecost. The people who were baptized were the lambs of the fold; the Apostles were their shepherds. They took care of them and taught them all that Jesus had told them to teach. Peter was their visible leader. He watched over the lambs and the sheep of the flock.

Now answer these questions:

1. Why were the Apostles together in the Upper Room?
2. Who was with them?
3. What happened after nine days?
4. How did the Holy Ghost come down?
5. Why did the people come running?
6. Who spoke to the people?
7. What strange thing happened while Peter spoke?
8. Did all the people believe what Peter was saying?
9. What feast do we celebrate in honor of the coming of the Holy Ghost?
10. How many were baptized on the first day?
11. Who was the shepherd of the new flock?

When the people of Jerusalem heard the words of Peter, they asked: "What shall we do?"

Our priests, teachers, and parents often speak to us about God and about the teachings of the Church. We must not only listen to their instructions, we must also do what they tell us.

Try to be very attentive during your religion lesson and see how many things you can do today that show by your actions that you are a good Christian boy or girl. Here are a few hints:

I know God is present on the altar in Church. I will *show* that I know it, by my good behavior at Mass.

I know that God sees and knows all things. I will remember that, when I am tempted to cheat or do wrong in school.

I know God has commanded me to love and obey my parents. I will *show* today that I wish to obey God's commandment.

I am alone and am tempted to steal. I will *show* that I wish to obey God by keeping away from temptation.

Now add other examples to show that good Christian boys or girls are known by their *actions*.

Things to do:

1. Find the story of Jesus ascending into heaven and tell the class about it.

2. Find when the Feast of Pentecost is this year and tell what color vestment the priest wears and why.

3. On the map find the places from which the Jews came to Jerusalem.

4. Imagine you are one of the people baptized by St. Peter. Write to a friend in another city and tell what you saw and heard.

5. The Holy Ghost is often pictured in the form of a dove. Look for this symbol in the windows and paintings of your church.

6. Memorize the seven gifts of the Holy Ghost. They are: Wisdom, Understanding, Counsel, Fortitude, Knowledge, Piety, Fear of the Lord.

7. Memorize the following Scripture text: "And they were all filled with the Holy Ghost, and they began to speak with divers tongues, according as the Holy Ghost gave them to speak" (Acts ii. 4).

8. Say a little prayer to the Holy Ghost when you need light and help: "Inflame our hearts with the fire of the Holy Spirit that we may serve Thee with chaste bodies and please Thee with clean hearts." Or, "Holy Spirit, enlighten me."

9. Read the story "King Robert of Sicily" and tell whether you think he acted and spoke as a good Christian king should.

Can you answer these questions?

1. Who is the Holy Ghost?

2. Who is the first Person of the Blessed Trinity?

3. Who is the second Person of the Blessed Trinity?

4. What is the Blessed Trinity?

5. Can we fully understand how the three Divine Persons can be one and the same God?

6. What is a mystery?

7. Which mystery of the Rosary reminds us of Pentecost?

8. When should we pray to the Holy Ghost?

9. Why should we pray to the Holy Ghost?

10. What sacraments bring the Holy Ghost into our souls?

11. What is baptism?

12. What is confirmation?

13. How do we know what God wants us to do?

Good things to read:

"The Beggar in the Beautiful Gate," *American Reader V,* page 19.

"King Robert of Sicily," *Shields Reader V,* page 81.

Test Yourself

Fill in the blanks with the missing words. Then see how many you have correct. If you get 20 points you have a perfect score.

1. I am the . . . ., you are the branches.

2. The Church was founded by . . . .

3. Jesus is the . . . . head of the Church.

4. All who are in heaven belong to the Church . . . .

5. The faithful on earth are the Church . . . .

6. The souls in purgatory are the Church . . . .

7. All three together are called . . . .

8. On the first of November we celebrate the Feast of . . . .

9. .... was the first pope.

10. The pope takes the place of .... on earth.

11. The pope is the .... head of the Church.

12. Our Holy Father today is Pope ....

13. The pope lives in that part of Rome called ....

14. The palace in which the pope lives is called the ....

15. The Holy Ghost came down from heaven on ....

16. Pentecost is the .... of the Church.

17. The Holy Ghost came upon the Apostles in the form of fiery ....

18. The priest wears a .... vestment on Pentecost day.

19. The Holy Ghost is the .... Person of the Blessed Trinity.

20. .... is the second Person of the Blessed Trinity.

UNIT II

The Growth of the Early Church

The Church began its great work in Jerusalem and from there spread over all parts of the world. But there were many people who did not want to be good or belong to the Church of Christ. They had hated Christ and crucified Him, and they hated His followers also. They tried their best to overthrow Christianity, but they did not succeed. Christ had promised that the gates of hell should not prevail against it.

The spread of the Church of Christ over the world is a story of great heroes and saints. The Apostles and disciples started the work on Pentecost day. From Jerusalem they went to preach the Gospel in other cities, then in other countries out beyond the sea. Nothing could stop them. They were hated and persecuted, and at last put to death. But where one died, a hundred and more Christians seemed to spring up, until it was said that the blood of the martyrs was the seed of Christianity.

We shall now hear of the wonderful spread of the faith all over the world and of the price Christ's followers had to pay before the victory was won.

4. St. Stephen, the First Martyr

There was great excitement among the Christians in Jerusalem. Stephen, the friend of the poor, was in the power of the Jewish leaders, who hated the Christians.

"And who is this Stephen," asked a passer-by, "that everybody is so concerned about him?"

"Don't you know? He is one of the seven deacons. These men go around with the Apostles and help them with their work of preaching to the people and feeding the poor."

"Well?"

"Everybody loves him. He has converted many to the Christian faith. Today he was accused of breaking the Jewish law. You should have heard him talking to the rulers. Why, he more than proved to them that Christ was the Promised Redeemer."

"The rulers do not seem to feel very good about it. Look at them now, pushing him out of the city gates. How they forget themselves in their anger."

"Poor Stephen! And yet, see how calm he is. He does not seem to see or hear them. Perhaps he is still looking into the heavens. A little while ago, when he stood before the Jewish Council, he said: 'Behold, I see the heavens opened and the Son of Man standing on the right hand of God!' That was too much for the rulers. It looks as if they are going to kill him."

And Stephen said: "Behold I see the heavens opened, and the Son of man standing on the right hand of God."

The two speakers were lost in the crowd that followed through the city gates. Soon there was a halt. There stood Stephen surrounded by the angry mob. A large stone struck him on the head; another and another followed. Stephen fell on his knees, still calm, still looking up to heaven. The blood was flowing down his face. "Lord Jesus, receive my spirit," he prayed aloud.

Somewhat away from the crowd a young man was holding the garments of those who were throwing stones at Stephen. He seemed well pleased with the work of the mob.

"You are glad that the Council is putting this man out of the way, Saul?"

Saul nodded. "It is time that he and his kind are sent where they can do no more harm. Oh, these hated Christians! To believe this Man Jesus to be the Son of God! To pray to a crucified God! It seems too terrible to believe."

He stopped. Everything had suddenly become very still. A voice that seemed to come from far away, pleaded: "Lord, lay not this sin to their charge."

A shower of stones followed. Stephen lay very quiet upon his face. Stephen, the first Christian martyr, had gone to his Lord.

Now answer these questions:
1. What was the work of the deacons?
2. Why was Stephen stoned?
3. What prayer did Stephen say for those who stoned him?

4. What was the name of the young man who watched the men's garments?

5. What were Stephen's last words?

*   *   *

Do you know of anyone else who prayed for His enemies when He was dying? What were His words? How do you feel or act toward those who hurt or hate you?

What would you do?

1. St. Stanislaus and his brother were going to school far away from home. Stanislaus was treated shamefully by his brother and even beaten and kicked. If you had been in St. Stanislaus' place, what would you have done? Read the life of St. Stanislaus and find how he acted.

2. John broke a window at home. His little brother Ben gets the blame. If you were Ben, what would you do?

3. St. John Gualbert met his greatest enemy on a narrow mountain pass. He had a good chance to kill the man. The man begged him in the name of Jesus to forgive the wrong he had done. If you were St. John Gualbert, what would you do? Read about St. John Gualbert and find out what happened.

4. St. Germaine was cruelly treated by her stepmother. She had to go out and tend the sheep in the coldest weather and got very little to eat. If you were St. Germaine, what would you do? Read her life and learn how she was rewarded by God.

5. You are walking along the street and a boy comes running past and accidentally pushes against you. What are you going to say if he comes to excuse himself?

6. You put an apple on the shelf at home. You want to eat it after school but find that your little brother ate it while you were gone. What are you going to do about it?

7. Anne and Betty are playing house. Anne breaks Betty's beautiful new doll. She did not mean to do it. Betty is your

little sister. She tells you about it and cries bitterly. What are you going to do for Betty?

8. There is a girl in your neighborhood who does not like you. Every time she gets a chance she makes faces at you or says mean things. You have never done anything to hurt her. One day while she is out roller skating she falls and hurts herself right outside of your house. No one sees her but you. What are you going to do?

Things to do:

1. On a Catholic calendar find the Feast of St. Stephen. What color vestment does the priest wear on that day? Why?

2. Dramatize the story of St. Stephen.

3. Write a play about St. John Gualbert meeting his enemy. His feast is celebrated on July 12. Look for it on the calendar.

4. Find a story in one of your readers about someone who returned good for evil.

5. Learn the words which Jesus said about loving our enemies: "Love your enemies; do good to them that hate you, and pray for them that persecute and calumniate you" (Matt. v. 44).

6. In the Our Father Jesus teaches us that we should forgive our enemies. Find the sentence.

7. Say the Spiritual Works of Mercy and tell which of them remind you of the lesson for today.

8. What stories in the Old Testament show forgiveness of enemies? Tell the class about one of them.

Can you answer these questions?

1. Why should we love our enemies?

2. How can we show love for our enemies?

3. Against what commandment did the Jews sin by killing St. Stephen?

4. What is the fifth commandment?

5. What does the fifth commandment forbid?
6. How must we take care of our own bodies?
7. Why must we take care of our own bodies?

Good things to read:

"The Heart of a Priest," *American Cardinal Reader V*, page 134.

"The Passion of Our Lord," *American Cardinal Reader V*, page 296.

"St. Stanislaus," *Misericordia Reader V*, page 36.

"For Greater Things," *American Reader V*, page 157.

"St. Stephen, the First Martyr," *Ideal Reader V*, page 97.

5. Who Art Thou, Lord?

A party of horsemen is leaving the gates of Jerusalem. They are in a hurry to be on their way. They must find all the hated Christians and stop them before they carry their teachings any farther. Already these disciples of Christ have spread out beyond Jerusalem as far as the city of Damascus. But now they would be surprised and brought to justice. Saul, the leader of the party, would make sure of that. He had letters from the high priest of the Jews, giving him the power to arrest and bring them back to Jerusalem in chains.

We have met Saul before. It is the same young man who watched the garments of those who had stoned the holy deacon Stephen.

Saul was an eager and bright student of the Jewish

Law. It was because he honestly believed that Stephen and the other followers of Jesus were enemies of that Law, that he wanted to destroy them. That is why we find him now on his way to Damascus to capture them.

The horsemen are nearing the city. All of a sudden, out of a clear sky, comes a flash of blinding light. Saul is struck to the ground. He hears a voice: "Saul, Saul, why dost thou persecute Me?"

"Who art Thou, Lord?" asks Saul.

"I am Jesus, whom thou persecutest," comes the answer.

Jesus! The crucified God of the Christians! Saul trembles.

"Lord, what wilt Thou have me do?" he asks.

"Arise, and go into the city, and there it shall be told thee what to do."

When Saul arose, he could not see. He was led into the city, where he spent three days fasting and praying.

Then the Lord appeared to a Christian by the name of Ananias and said:

"Go and look for a man named Saul of Tarsus. For behold, he prayeth. I have chosen him to carry My name to the Gentiles and kings and the children of Israel. I will show him what great things he must suffer for My name's sake."

Ananias went, and laying his hands upon Saul's head, said: "Brother Saul, the Lord sent me that you may be filled with the Holy Ghost and receive your sight."

Something like scales fell from Saul's eyes, and he

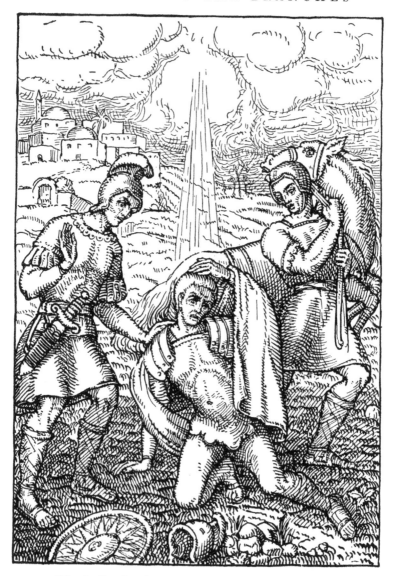

"Saul, Saul, why dost thou persecute Me?"

could see once more. He was baptized and from that time on was as eager to preach the gospel of Christ as he had been to persecute the Christians. He was now called Paul.

For three years Paul lived in a desert and prepared himself for his work. Then he went to St. Peter and offered his help for the spread of the Faith.

In all the history of the Church, no one ever labored with more zeal for the spread of the Church than Paul. With Barnabas and other companions he set out on his missionary journey. At first he tried to convert the Jews, but when he saw how these men hardened their hearts against the teachings of Christ, he turned to the Gentiles, who received the gospel with joy.

Wherever Paul went, he founded Christian communities or parishes. When he was ready to go on, he left priests and bishops behind to stay with the new members of the Church and to instruct them further. So he went from city to city and out beyond the sea to distant countries and islands, to Rome and perhaps even to Spain. How much he went through for the love of Christ, he himself tells us:

"Of the Jews five times did I receive forty stripes, save one.

"Thrice was I beaten with rods, once I was stoned; thrice I suffered shipwreck, a night and a day I was in the depth of the sea.

"In journeying often, in perils of waters, in perils of robbers, in perils from my own nation, in perils from the

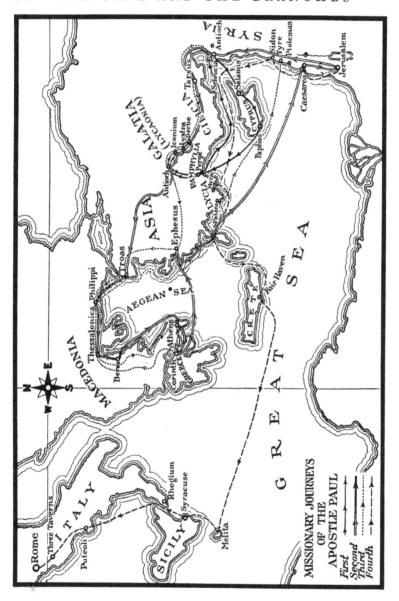

Gentiles, in perils in the city, in perils in the wilderness, in perils in the sea, in perils from false brethren.

"In labor and painfulness, in much watchings, in hunger and thirst, in fastings often, in cold and nakedness."

But nothing was too much for him. His only thought was to make Christ known all over the world. Twice he returned from long journeys, only to set out again for new and farther countries to conquer. Was there ever a more victorious conqueror the world over? And all the while he was earning his own bread by the work of his hands. What courage and what love must have burned in the heart of Paul to work and suffer so much for Christ.

At last Paul reached the end of his journey on earth. He was taken prisoner and brought to Rome. He had spent much of his life preaching Christ crucified. Now he was to have the honor to shed his blood for Him. Glorious Paul!

In the great city of Rome, Paul, the Apostle of the Gentiles, the great lover of Christ, was beheaded in the year A.D. 69. It was probably on the same day and in the same city, that St. Peter, the first pope, was crucified.

Now answer these questions:
1. What did Saul intend to do in Damascus?
2. What happened on the way?
3. Who struck Saul to the ground?
4. What did Saul ask the Lord?
5. Who was sent to help Saul?

6. What was Saul afterwards called?
7. How many journeys did Paul make?
8. Who was his companion at first?
9. Why did he make these journeys?
10. Why did he not continue to preach to the Jews?
11. What did he suffer?
12. When did he die?
13. How did he die?
14. Who else probably died on the same day?

Is there any country in the world now where there are few or no Christians? Does the Church do anything today, to spread the faith? What?

Can you do anything to help spread the faith?

Pray today for the missionaries who are working so hard to save souls for Christ.

Things to do:

1. Write as many ways as you can think of in which you can help to make the faith known to others.

2. Make a mission scrapbook. In it put all the mission pictures you can find.

3. If you do not get the *Little Missionary* or *The Field Afar* send for a copy and show it to the class.

4. Find the journeys of St. Paul on the map and name some of the cities in which he stopped.

5. The feasts of SS. Peter and Paul are celebrated on the same day. Find the date of the feast. What color vestment does the priest wear on that day? Why?

6. Find the Feast of the Conversion of St. Paul in January.

7. St. Paul wrote fourteen letters or epistles to the Christians. In the Holy Bible find to whom some of these letters were written.

8. Find out what you can about the Holy Childhood Association. If you are not a member, perhaps you can become one. That would be one good way of helping to spread the faith.

9. In the lesson is a beautiful sentence which you could use as a prayer to ask God what He would like you to be when you grow up. Find the sentence.

10. Find stories about great missionaries in our own country and tell about one of them to the class.

11. Bring mission pictures to put on the bulletin board.

12. See whether there is a picture or statue of St. Paul in your church. What does he hold? Why?

13. Read the lives of St. Peter and some of the other Apostles to learn about their work and sufferings.

14. One Apostle did not die a martyr's death and yet he is honored as a martyr. Can you find who it is?

15. Look for the feasts of the different Apostles on the calendar.

16. Memorize the following words of St. Paul: "I have fought the good fight, I have finished my course, I have kept the faith. Henceforth there is laid up for me the crown of justice which the Lord, the just Judge, will render to me in that day; and not only to me, but to them also that love His coming" (II Tim. iv. 6–8).

Can you answer these questions?

1. Why did the Apostles go out to teach?

2. Who gave them the right?

3. What prayer contains all the chief truths of the Catholic religion?

4. What book contains the inspired word of God which all must believe?

5. What is meant by fasting?

6. Why must people fast?

7. Who must fast?

8. What can you do instead of fasting?

Good things to read:

"San of the Cross," *Misericordia Reader V,* page 18.

"The Conversion of Saul," *American Reader V,* page 36.

"A Maryknoll Missioner," *American Reader V,* page 167.

"St. Paul," *Literature and Art IV.*

6. Timothy, Beloved Disciple of St. Paul

"Mother, do you remember the cripple that always sat in the square to beg?"

Timothy was all excitement as he ran into the garden where his mother was gathering roses.

"Yes, my son, I know him well. He has been lame for many years."

"He can walk, mother!"

Timothy stopped for want of breath. His mother smiled, but went on with her work. "Two strangers came into the city this morning," he went on, "to talk to the people in the square. Men say they are gods. They cannot be gods, mother, can they? In the book from which you read to me it says there is only one God who is in heaven."

Timothy's mother stopped suddenly.

"Come, let us see," she said.

Throwing her mantle about her, she followed her son

to the square. There were the two strange men, and with them the former cripple, now as straight as a young tree. One of the strangers was preaching about the Messias. Timothy's mother knew about the Messias; for although she lived in Lystra, a pagan land, she was a Jewess and often read the Scripture. Her heart was glad. She would stay and learn more.

The sermon was soon interrupted, however.

"The priests are at the city gate with oxen and garlands," someone shouted. "Come, let us sacrifice to these two strangers. They are surely gods come down to us in the likeness of men." And a great shout arose among the people, who made ready to go to the sacrifice.

When the chief speaker heard these words, he cried out to the people:

"Why do you do these things? We are men like you, preaching the living God who made the heaven and the earth and the sea and all things that are in them." But he had a hard time to make the people understand that sacrifice must not be offered to them.

Timothy's mother invited the two men to stay at her home. There she learned that her guests were the great Paul himself and his companion the Apostle Barnabas. Soon Timothy and his mother and grandmother became Christians. Every day they listened to the Apostles' stories about Christ, His suffering and death, and about the Church He founded to save men.

"Mother," Timothy said one day, "I, too, wish to

preach the Gospel with Paul." But Paul said he would have to wait.

"I will be back again, my son; and then you may come with me," he promised.

From that day on, Timothy longed more and more to be a missionary with Paul. He prayed and studied very hard, so that he would be ready when Paul came. Often, too, he would go out along the road, hoping to meet the Apostle on the way.

One year passed, and then another and another, but Paul did not come. Timothy had grown to be a tall, handsome young man, with a soul so pure that God and the angels must have looked on it with pleasure.

At last, after seven years, news came that Paul was on his way again to Lystra. Timothy and his mother went out with the other Christians of the city to meet him. Paul hardly knew the splendid young man before him. But soon he learned from the inhabitants of Lystra of the pious and noble life Timothy had been leading. We may well imagine the joy of all the people and of the mother and the son, when Paul laid his hands upon the young man and made him a priest of God.

From that time on Timothy became the beloved friend and companion of Paul. He went with him to help spread the teachings of Christ over the world.

He was finally left at Ephesus as bishop of the Christian community. Here he received two letters or epistles from St. Paul. The last one of these epistles was written by Paul from his prison in Rome. In it he tells of his sufferings and asks Timothy to come to him once more before he dies.

Not many years after the death of St. Paul, Timothy himself won the martyr's crown. From his childhood he had gladly listened to the instructions of his mother and later of St. Paul. No wonder he was found worthy to become a bishop in the early Church, a leader of his people, and a follower of Christ even to the shedding of his blood.

Now answer these questions:

1. Who were the two strangers that came to Lystra?
2. Why did they come?
3. What miracle did Paul perform?
4. For whom did the pagans take them?
5. What were they going to do?
6. How long did Timothy have to wait for Paul's return?
7. What did Paul hear about Timothy at Lystra?
8. What did Paul do for Timothy?
9. What work did Timothy do for the Church?
10. By what name are the letters of St. Paul called?
11. Where was Paul when he wrote his last letter to Timothy?
12. What death did Timothy die?

* * *

Timothy was prepared for his great missionary work with St. Paul, by leading a good life and by reading the Scriptures. God has a special work or vocation for all of us. We must prepare ourselves for this work by leading a good life and also by reading good books, especially the Scriptures.

The Scriptures, also called the Holy Bible, are the word of God. They are divided into the Old and the New Testament.

Things to do:

1. The Holy Bible is really made up of 72 smaller books all bound in one. The first book is called the Book of Genesis. It tells about the creation of the world. You will be interested to read the first part. Read it with reverence as you would a prayer.

2. Look at the Holy Bible and find the Old Testament and the New Testament. Sometimes the Old and New Testament are each printed in a separate book.

3. Toward the end of the Bible, you will find the letters or epistles written by the Apostles. Look for the two epistles written to Timothy and tell how St. Paul starts the letters.

4. Find out whether you have a Holy Bible in your home. If it is a Catholic Bible it will have the word *Imprimatur* on the inside of the title-page, and the name of a bishop or an archbishop near it. See whether you can find this word. It means *it may be printed.* Somewhere on the title-page you will also find the words *Douay Version.* That tells you that this Bible is one approved by the bishops of the Catholic Church.

5. The Scripture texts in your book always tell from what part of the Bible the lines were taken. Learn how to find these texts in the Bible and look for at least five of the texts from your book.

6. Find the Feast of St. Timothy. Do you know without looking at the calendar, what color vestment the priest wears on the feast? Why?

7. Imagine that you are Timothy and that you are making your first journey with St. Paul. Write home to your mother and tell her about your adventures.

8. Write a play about the cure of the cripple at Lystra.

Can you answer these questions?

1. What is the Holy Bible?
2. Into how many parts is the Holy Bible divided?
3. How many books has it?
4. What does the Old Testament contain? The New Testament?
5. Why would Paul and Barnabas not allow the people of Lystra to offer sacrifice to them?
6. What commandment forbids us to give to creatures the honor that belongs to God?
7. What are the sins committed against this commandment?
8. Does this commandment forbid us to honor the saints?
9. Are we allowed to pray to crucifixes or to images and relics of the saints?
10. Can the saints hear us?

Good things to read:

"Caedmon, One of the Great Poets," *American Reader V,* page 154.

"The Cowherd's Song," *Rosary Reader V,* page 365.

"Jesus Heals Two Blind Men," *Ideal Reader V,* page 266.

7. The Seed of Christianity

City of Rome, in the reign of Nero, the Emperor

Marcellus to Lucius Marcus:

You ought to be very glad that you no longer live in Rome. Mother says that never have things looked quite so dark as now. A short time ago a great fire started near the Circus Maximus. It lasted for days and burned down a large part of the city. It was a terrible sight. At night brother Claudius and I stood on the roof of our villa and watched the bright red flames leap up to the sky.

No one knows just how the fire started, but soon it began to be whispered about that Nero, our august emperor himself, caused the fire. Nero, however, blamed the Christians and had a number of them thrown into prison. They were tortured until some said that they were guilty. What happened after that is almost too terrible to tell. The Christians were dragged out of their houses and put to death. Some were covered with the skins of animals and thrown to the hungry dogs. Some were put on the rack and torn to pieces. Many were led into the circus to be devoured by tigers, lions, or panthers. But I think the most terrible thing happened in the gardens of Nero. Men and women were smeared with pitch and tied on high posts. At night while the emperor was feasting, they were set on fire so that they might serve as human torches.

Father says it is wonderful with what joy these people go to their death. It almost makes him feel as if their teachings must be true. Today he told us that the two great leaders of the Christians, men by the names of Peter and Paul, are in prison and will probably have to die. When mother heard the news, she looked very sad. Afterwards I saw that she had been weeping.

Some day I hope father will let me go along to the

prison to see these strange people who smile and sing in spite of their cruel sufferings. I do not believe the many wicked things people say about them. Father says it takes a noble heart to face hard things bravely; and father is a great soldier and ought to know.

Are there any Christians in Athens? Flavia, one of our slaves, says they have spread all over the world.

Tell me all about yourself and your home in Greece. Farewell, Lucius Marcus.

Your friend,
Marcellus

Now answer these questions:
1. Where did the great fire of Rome start?
2. What was whispered about in the city after the fire?
3. How were the Christians treated?
4. How did they bear their sufferings?
5. What two great leaders were in prison?

*   *   *

The martyrs gave their lives for their faith because they knew that faith is the most precious gift of God. They suffered terrible things rather than offend God. Are you willing to suffer anything for Jesus? Do you try very hard not to offend Him by sin? When you read the lives of the martyrs, ask yourself how much you would be willing to suffer for your faith!

Thank God today for having given you the gift of Faith and promise Him that you, too, will die rather than ever give it up.

Things to do:

1. Read the story of a Christian martyr and tell the class about it.

2. Dramatize the story of one of the martyrs.

3. Find the city of Rome on the map.

4. Imagine that you are Lucius Marcus who lives in Athens. Answer the letter of Marcellus.

5. Write a letter from Rome telling about the death of St. Peter or St. Paul.

6. The city of Athens is in Greece. Find it on the map.

7. Read about the catacombs and tell the class about an imaginary visit to one of them.

8. Tell the class what kind of boy you imagine Marcellus to be.

9. Make a booklet, "My Favorite Saints," and in it write about the saints whose stories you read and wish to keep. Also find pictures of these saints for your booklet. In Catholic magazines and newspapers you will often find sayings of the saints. Watch for them and copy those that fit into your saint booklet. Make your booklet as beautiful as you can.

10. Learn one of the following Scripture texts:

"Without faith it is impossible to please God."

"Amen, Amen, I say unto you, he that believeth in Me, hath everlasting life."

Can you answer these questions?

1. What is faith?
2. How can you show your faith?
3. When did you receive the gift of faith?
4. What other gifts did you receive at the same time?
5. How do we sin against faith?
6. How do we sin against hope?
7. How do we sin against charity or love?

8. Make an act of faith, hope, and charity.
9. What is baptism?
10. What does baptism do for the soul?
11. Who may baptize?
12. How do you baptize?
13. What name did you receive in baptism? Why?
14. What do you know about your patron saint?
15. What promise did your godparents make for you in baptism?
16. Who are your godparents?
17. Have they any duties toward you?

Good things to read:

"The Price of Faith," *American V*, page 14.
"Pancratius," *Catholic National V*.
"St. Cecelia — a Martyr," *Catholic National V*.
"Prisca's Courage," *Marywood Reader V*, page 226.
"The Story of Tarcisius," *De La Salle Reader V*, page 163.
"The Martyr's Boy," *De La Salle Reader V*, page 237.
"St. Dorothy, Martyr," *De La Salle Reader V*, page 207.

8. Augustine, Sinner and Saint

"Do not weep, my good woman. A son whose mother sheds so many tears and prays so much for him. cannot be lost forever."

It was a bishop who spoke these words to Monica, the mother of Augustine. Her heart was sad because her only son would not listen to her words and live the life of a Christian. But she remembered what the good bishop had said, and for twenty years continued to pray

St. Augustine and his Mother.

that her son might change his sinful ways and be converted.

One day an officer at the home of Augustine related the story of a man who had given up all his wealth and gone to live in the desert.

"And why did he do such a foolish thing?" Augustine wanted to know.

"He gave up everything," the officer answered, "so that he might gain heaven."

Augustine was struck by the answer.

"These simple men," he said, "take heaven by force; they do so much to gain heaven, and we, who are supposed to be learned and should therefore know better, do not even want to serve God and be saved." He went out into the garden to think.

"How long are you going to put off your conversion," a voice within him said. "Why not start right now?"

"Shall I or shall I not?" Augustine asked himself over and over again.

A fresh young voice was singing somewhere: "Take and read, take and read." On the table lay the Holy Scripture.

Augustine opened the roll and read a few sentences which began: "Walk honestly as in the day." It was enough for him. Going to his mother, he said:

"Mother, from now on my life will be different."

And so it was. Augustine was baptized by St. Ambrose at the age of 34. He gave all he had to the poor, changed his sinful ways, and began to lead the life of a saint. He became a priest and later a bishop. All his time was spent in preaching and in working for God and His Church.

At that time there were many Christians who believed things which were not according to the teachings of the Church. Such false teachings are called heresy, and one who teaches them is called a heretic. No one knew better how to preach against heresy than the great St. Augustine, because he himself had been a heretic before his conversion.

For 35 years St. Augustine was a shining light in the Church. He wrote many books to help the early Christians in their religion and brought many heretics back to the faith. He was known throughout the Christian world as one of its great teachers and saints.

The story is told that one day St. Augustine was walking along the seashore thinking very deeply. He was trying hard to understand the mystery of the Holy Trinity. But the more he thought, the less he could understand. All at once he saw a beautiful boy playing in the sand. With a shell the boy was carrying some water from the sea to a little hole on the shore.

"What are you doing, my boy?" asked St. Augustine.

"I am going to put all the water from the sea into this hole," the boy answered.

"But, my child," Augustine said, "can you not see that you will not be able to do that? The sea is much too large for that little hole."

The boy looked straight at the saint, deep into his

soul. Then, with a voice which Augustine could never forget, he answered:

"Augustine, as impossible as it is for me to get the great sea into this little hole, so impossible is it to get into your little human mind the great mysteries of God."

Then the child disappeared. Augustine was satisfied. He knew that God is too great to be understood by man.

The saint died in the year 430 after he had built up a strong Christian community in Northern Africa. He is known as one of the Fathers of the Church. It was the prayers of a good mother that gave the Church this wonderful saint.

Now answer these questions:
1. Who was the mother of St. Augustine?
2. How long did she pray for his conversion?
3. From what book did Augustine read in the garden?
4. Who is a heretic?
5. What did Augustine do for the Church?
6. What was he trying to think of on the seashore?
7. What did the little boy tell him?
8. By what title is St. Augustine known?

*   *   *

To be honored by the title "Father of the Church" four things are necessary:
1. The person must have lived while the Church was still young; that is, in the first centuries of Christianity.
2. He must have led a saintly life.
3. His writing must have been free from all heresy and must have explained and defended the Catholic religion.
4. His writings must have been approved by the Church.

Among the saints who received the title "Father of the Church" are St. Justin, martyr, and St. Clement of Alexandria. Read their lives and tell why they deserved the title.

St. Augustine is often pictured with a heart in his hand, because he spoke the beautiful words: "Our hearts are restless until they rest in Thee, O Lord." What do these words mean? That we shall never be satisfied with the things of this world alone. We shall always be looking for something greater and higher, and we shall never be happy until we belong entirely to God. Memorize the words.

There are other saints who later received the title "Doctor of the Church" because their writings contained important religious teachings. Do you know any of the following saints? They are all Doctors of the Church. Choose seven pupils to tell the class something interesting about each of them. The number after each name tells the year of the saint's death.

St. Ambrose, bishop of Milan, 397.

St. Jerome, priest, 420.

St. Gregory, the Great, pope, 604.

St. Athanasius, bishop of Alexandria, 373.

St. Basil, bishop of Cæsarea, 379.

St. Gregory Nazianzen, 389.

St. John Chrysostom, bishop of Constantinople, 407.

Can you answer these questions?

1. Why were we created?

2. What words of St. Augustine are an answer to the first question?

3. Why could Augustine not understand the Trinity?

4. In what short prayers do we use the names of the Trinity?

5. To whom did St. Augustine owe his conversion?

6. What did his mother do for his conversion?

7. What is prayer?

8. Is prayer necessary for us? Why?
9. Which is the greatest prayer of all? Why?
10. What other prayers can you say?
11. For whom should we pray?
12. When should we pray?
13. How should we pray?
14. How should we behave during prayer?

Good things to read:

"St. Monica," *Heroes of God's Church*, page 42.
"The Thought of God," *Ideal Reader V*, page 142.
"Two Messages," *Ideal Reader V*, page 254.

9. The Victory of the Cross

For three hundred years the Roman emperors tried their best to put an end to Christianity. At last Emperor Diocletian was sure he had succeeded. He even had a coin made on which it said: "Diocletian, who destroyed Christianity." But the blood of the martyrs was the seed of Christianity. The more Christians that gave up their lives, the more Christians seemed to spring up all around.

It was the year 312. Constantine, at the head of an army of 25,000 men, was marching against his enemy, Maxentius. Although not a Christian himself, Constantine was kind to those who worshiped Christ. The Christians loved him in return and prayed that he might win the victory.

One day when Constantine was nearing Rome, he saw a cross of light in the heavens, and around it the words: "In this sign thou shalt conquer." At once he put the cross on his standard in place of the Roman Eagle and, trusting in the help of God, marched on.

In Rome the pagan priests offered sacrifice to the idols for Maxentius. His army was much larger. He was not afraid. He trusted in the help of the gods.

Crossing over the Tiber River with his great army, Maxentius ordered his soldiers to weaken one of the bridges so that Constantine and his men would drown if they tried to cross it. The two armies met. There was a terrible battle. In the end the soldiers of Maxentius fled in wild disorder over the same bridge which they expected Constantine to cross. The bridge gave way and thousands of men drowned in the Tiber. Among them was Maxentius.

Constantine marched into Rome in triumph. From that day on the Christians were free to worship God openly. Constantine himself later became a Christian.

Soon there was a great change in Rome. There were Christians everywhere; and where there are Christians, there the cross has the place of honor. In time the cross could be seen on the churches that were being built everywhere. The cross shone on top of the former temples of the god Jupiter, which became temples of the true God. The cross was the standard of the army and the sign of hope and peace for all people. The cross, which was formerly a sign of shame, became a sign of honor.

Constantine saw a cross of light in the heavens, and
the words: "In this sign thou shalt conquer."

Now answer these questions:

1. For how many years did the Roman emperors try to put an end to Christianity?
2. What emperor thought he had destroyed Christianity?
3. Who was the first emperor to become a Christian?
4. Why did he take the cross as his standard?
5. Why was Maxentius not afraid to fight Constantine?
6. Who won the victory?
7. What change could be seen in Rome after Constantine's victory?

*   *   *

The sign of the cross is a symbol of our faith. Do you make the sign of the cross with reverence? Is there a crucifix in your home? Has it a place of honor?

There is a difference between a cross and a crucifix. The crucifix has an image of our Lord's body on it and the cross has not. The word *crucifix* comes from two Latin words, *cruci* and *fixus,* which mean "fixed to a cross."

There are crosses of different shapes and names. Find the shapes of the following crosses, cut them out of colored paper and mount them on large sheets with the proper explanation under each cross. Clasp the sheets together and make a book, with the word *Crosses* on the cover. Whenever you find something interesting about the cross add it to your book. By and by you will have a valuable collection.

Here are the names of some of the crosses you should look for:

Latin cross   Celtic cross
Greek cross   Egyptian cross
St. Andrew's cross   Tau cross
Maltese cross   Patriarchal cross
                    Russian cross

Things to do:

1. Make a picture of the cross as you think it appeared to Constantine and around it write the words: "In this sign thou shalt conquer."

2. Draw the standard which Constantine used at the head of the army.

3. Look around you today and see in how many places you can find a crucifix.

4. Draw and cut out the coin of Diocletian. On one side print the words "Diocletian, who destroyed Christianity," and on the other draw a picture of Diocletian. Tell the story.

5. There are two feasts of the Holy Cross. Find them on the calendar.

6. Find out the meaning of the letters I N R I often found on top of a crucifix.

7. During twelve days of the year all crucifixes in church are covered. Find out when and why.

Can you answer these questions?

1. Why do we make the sign of the cross?

2. What mystery does the sign of the cross remind us of?

3. When should we make the sign of the cross?

4. On what day of the year do Catholics go to church and kiss the crucifix? Why?

5. The cross is a sacramental. What is a sacramental?

6. Name some of the sacramentals.

7. What is the difference between a sacrament and a sacramental?

Good things to read:

"The Cross and the Crucifix," *Catholic Youth Reader V*, page 39.

"The Stations of the Cross," *Catholic Youth Reader V*, page 437.

10. To Nicæa, to Meet in Council

Never had the city of Nicæa in Asia Minor seen so much splendor and excitement. Every day more strangers were coming in. And they were not ordinary men, these strangers, but great leaders of the Church: bishops, priests, and deacons. Among them were men who suffered during the persecutions. There was one with his right eye gone, another with crippled hands, still others with fingers or arms cut off. They came from north and south, from east and west, to meet in the palace of the emperor. Several priests arrived from Rome. One of them was to take the place of the pope, who was too old to travel. Emperor Constantine himself was also there. It was, indeed, a wonderful meeting.

And why did all these great men of the Christian world come together? Many years before, when the Apostles had had questions about the affairs of the Church, which they could not settle alone, they all met in Jerusalem. This first meeting was known as the Council of Jerusalem. It was held in the year 49. Looking on St. Peter as their head, the Apostles talked things over, and with the help of the Holy Ghost decided what to do.

Now, too, in the year 325, there were important questions to be settled. False teachings had been spreading among the Christians. Such false teachings are called heresy, as we know. A priest had preached the heresy that Jesus Christ was only a man and not at the same time God. Many believed this heresy. Therefore it was decided that all the great teachers of Christianity, especially the bishops, should meet at Nicæa and settle these questions. And that is how it happened that so many of the world's greatest men came together in one place in spite of the fact that there were no cars or trains or steamers to make travel safe and easy.

We can picture that glorious meeting in the palace of the emperor. At the head sits the priest who came in place of the pope. All around him sit the bishops, 318 in number, the priests and the deacons, listening to the speakers or rising to speak themselves.

The meeting lasted many weeks. In order to make sure that all people would understand just what God and His Church wanted them to believe, a creed was written. All who were present had to sign this creed to show that they believed all that it contained. Because this creed was written in the city of Nicæa it was called the Nicene Creed. It is the Creed that you hear recited by the priest or sung by the choir during Mass on certain days.

Since the time of the meeting at Nicæa, there have been many other such gatherings. Whenever there were any questions or difficulties about a teaching of religion, the pope called the bishops of the world together. Such a meeting is called a General Council. Whatever the pope and bishops decide at such a council, about the teachings of religion, must be believed by all who wish to belong to the Catholic Church. Christ promised that He would be with His Church to the end of the world and watch over her so that she would teach nothing but what is true.

Now answer these questions:

1. How many bishops met in the city of Nicæa?
2. Why did all the bishops meet?
3. Who was the emperor at the meeting?
4. Why was the pope not there?
5. What did all who were present have to sign?
6. Why did they have to sign it?
7. What is such a meeting called in which all the bishops decide about the teachings of the Church?
8. Why can the Church not teach anything wrong?

What do you say?

1. Jim's father is not a Catholic. He says it does not make any difference whether you belong to the Catholic Church or to another, as long as you are good. Jim asks you about it. What do you say?

2. Ellen is staying with her grandma, who is not a Catholic. Grandma tells her that if the weather is not very pleasant on Sunday, she should stay in bed and not go to Mass. She says God did not say in the Bible that people had to hear Mass on Sunday. How should Ellen explain?

3. Bennie lives in St. Louis. His cousin Ed from Chicago is visiting with him. In church the priest announces that people in the parish should not go to see a movie which is just being shown. Ed says everybody went to see it in Chicago and the priest said nothing about it. "I thought the Church teaches the same thing everywhere," says Ed. What would you answer if you were in Bennie's place?

*   *   *

The Creed is not said at every Mass but just on Sunday

and certain other days. How can you tell whether the priest says the Creed? If you do not know, ask your teacher.

Learn the following Scripture text:

"And Jesus coming, spoke to them saying: All power is given to Me in heaven and on earth. Going therefore, teach ye all nations: baptizing them in the name of the Father, and of the Son, and of the Holy Ghost. Teaching them to observe all things whatsoever I have commanded you: and behold I am with you all days, even to the consummation of the world."

What powers did Jesus give to the Apostles and their successors by these words?

Which of these powers did the Council of Nicæa make use of?

Read the Nicene Creed carefully and say it at the same time with the priest at Mass.

Can you answer these questions?

1. What creed do you know?
2. What does it contain?
3. Who gave the Church the power to teach?
4. Does the Church teach the same thing at all times?
5. Is the teaching of the Catholic Church in China the same as in our country?
6. What are the false teachings of religion called?
7. Can the Church make a mistake when she tells Catholics what they must believe?
8. Who is at the head when a General Council meets?

The Nicene Creed

The Nicene Creed is said on Sundays, on feasts of our Lord and of our Lady, of the Apostles and of Doctors of the Church:

I believe in one God, the Father Almighty, maker of heaven and earth, and of all things visible and invisible. And in one Lord Jesus Christ, the only-begotten Son of God, born of the Father before all ages; God of God, light of light, true God of true God; begotten not made; consubstantial with the Father; by whom all things were made. Who for us men, and for our salvation, came down from heaven; (the celebrant genuflects and adores the Word made flesh) AND WAS INCARNATE BY THE HOLY GHOST, OF THE VIRGIN MARY; AND WAS MADE MAN. He was crucified also for us, suffered under Pontius Pilate, and was buried. And the third day He rose again according to the Scriptures; and ascended into heaven. He sitteth at the right hand of the Father; and He shall come again with glory to judge the living and the dead; and His Kingdom shall have no end. And in the Holy Ghost, the Lord and giver of life, who proceedeth from the Father and the Son, who together with the Father and the Son is adored and glorified; who spoke by the Prophets. And one holy, catholic, and apostolic Church. I confess one baptism for the remission of sins. And I await the resurrection of the dead (make the sign of the Cross), and the life of the world to come. Amen.

Test Yourself

Who are these saints? Ten points is a perfect score.

1. The saint who prayed twenty years for the conversion of her son. . . . .

2. The Apostle who first saw Jesus on the shore of the sea of Galilee.   . . . .

3. The saint who was with St. Paul when the people wanted to sacrifice to them.   . . . .

4. The saint who is represented with a heart in his hand.   . . . .

5. The saint who baptized St. Augustine.   . . . .

6. The saint who was ordained by St. Paul and became his companion missionary.   . . . .

7. The saint who was the first pope.   . . . .

8. The saint who was stoned to death.   . . . .

9. The two saints who, besides St. Augustine, are called "Fathers of the Church."   . . . . and . . . .

UNIT III

Hidden Heroes of Christ's Church

We know that thousands and thousands of Christians gave up their lives for the faith during the terrible persecutions in the first three centuries of Christianity.

There were others, however, who fled far into the desert to lead a quiet life away from all the noise and trouble of the world. In time they came to love this hidden life so well, that they did not care to leave it again. They found out how sweet it is to live alone with God and to spend the time in meditation and prayer, in penance and work. By and by others heard about the lives of these holy men and came to learn from them. At first each one built himself a little hut or hermitage and lived alone; but later they came to live together under one roof. They chose one man as their superior and obeyed him in everything. That was the beginning of a new kind of life called "Monastic Life." A man who lived in a monastery or convent was called a monk, which means "one who lives alone."

In the following stories we shall hear about some of the monks who became great saints by hiding away from the world and living alone with God.

11. Anthony Becomes a Hermit

It was the time of Holy Mass. Anthony, a young man who lived in Upper Egypt, was listening attentively to the words of the gospel: "If thou wilt be perfect, go, sell what thou hast, and give to the poor." The words went straight to his heart.

"Lord," he prayed, "I wish to be perfect. I will do as You say."

Anthony went home and sold everything that he had. He gave one half of the money to the poor, and left the other half for the education of his little sister. Then he went away to learn from an old hermit how to lead a holy life. Later he went into the desert and lived alone in an old ruin, where he prayed and fasted and worked for twenty years. He lived on bread and water and often knelt in prayer during the whole night. The devils, who could not bear to see so holy a man, often troubled him a great deal. But Anthony was not afraid. He said to them: "I fear you not; you cannot separate me from the love of Christ."

By and by many people came to Anthony for advice and some asked to stay near him so that they, too, might learn to become more perfect. In this way it happened that a large number of men came to live in huts or caves, with St. Anthony as their guide. This was the beginning of monastic or convent life. Like their holy superior the monks not only prayed and fasted but also worked. While their hearts were with God in prayer, their hands were busy making mats and baskets, paper and linen. Whatever they did not need themselves, they sent to the city to be sold. Every day on the Nile River one little boat could be seen on its way to the city carrying the goods which the monks had made, and another on its way back.

More and more people came to live near the good St. Anthony. The saint, however, loved best of all to be alone. One day he could not be found. He had gone away in order that he might once more lead the life of a hermit. And so he worked and prayed until he died at the age of 105. He had done his best to become perfect, as he had made up his mind to do many years before. Surely, God and the angels must have received him with great joy.

St. Anthony is called the Father of all Monks.

Now answer these questions:
1. Where did St. Anthony live?
2. What words of the gospel made Anthony sell all he had?
3. How long did Anthony live alone in the desert?
4. Why did many people come to him by and by?
5. What did the monks do all day?
6. Why did the saint go away from the monastery?
7. How old was St. Anthony when he died?
8. What is St. Anthony called?

*   *   *

Although St. Anthony did much penance and lived on bread and water, he became an old, old man. Penance is good for body and soul, if we are careful not to do anything that would harm us. Most people cannot do great penances, but there are many little penances that they can easily do. What penances can a boy or girl of your age do?

All of us must do penance for our sins either in this world or in the next. In confession the eternal punishment for our sins is taken away, but not the temporal punishment. God wants to teach us what a great evil sin is. Therefore we must make up or satisfy for the sins we have committed, by doing penance.

The following boys and girls are trying to do penance. See whether they are doing the right thing.

1. John is ten years old. He says he is not going to eat any meat for a whole month. John really does not like meat, but he is very fond of candy.

2. Ellen does not like to eat vegetables. She is going to eat more vegetables than she cares for.

3. Francis likes to stay in bed mornings and often comes late for school. His mother says it would be a good penance for him to get up at once when he is called. He says he is going to build a hermitage in the yard instead, and live out there part of the time, no matter how bad the weather is.

4. Gertrude spends ten cents a week for candy. One day she gets a terrible toothache and her sister tells her it is from eating too much candy. Gertrude makes up her mind to stop eating candy for a while. She thinks that will be a good penance for her.

5. Dan is sick in bed. He would like to have mother with him all the time, but he tries to stay alone for a while and tells God he will do so for penance.

6. Nellie does not like to help mother with the housework, but during Lent she is going to wipe the dishes every day without being asked.

7. Ben does not like to hear other pupils praised or see them rewarded. Now he makes up his mind to think kindly of everyone and to be glad with others when they are praised or rewarded.

8. Ed likes to eat every time he gets hold of something good. For a penance he is not going to eat between meals.

9. Eileen gets twenty-five cents and May five cents a week for spending money. They both put one cent a week in the mission bank.

10. Helen is praised by Sister for giving an apple to a poor child. After that Helen brings an apple every day and gives it to the poor child when Sister is around to see it.

11. For penance during Lent, Mollie, aged 11, is not going to drink any milk.

12. Della goes to Holy Communion every day. Sometimes she commits little faults during the day. She wants to make her heart as pure as possible for Jesus. What can she do, besides going to confession, to make her heart free from her little faults?

Things to do:

1. Make or draw a small hut or hermitage.

2. Memorize the words of the gospel which went straight to Anthony's heart.

3. Find out more about paper and the other articles mentioned and tell the class how you think the monks made them.

4. Locate the Nile River in Egypt and tell in what city the boats might have delivered the goods the monks made.

5. Cut out or draw the boats that went up the Nile River. Under them write the names of the articles they carried and by whom they were made.

6. Find the Feast of St. Anthony, the hermit, and tell what color vestment the priest wears at Mass. Why?

Can you answer these questions?

1. Why does God punish us for sin?
2. How can we satisfy or make up to God for temporal punishment due to sin?
3. Is all punishment for sin forgiven when we receive absolution?
4. How else is punishment forgiven?
5. Is penance harmful for us?
6. May we do any kind of penance?

Good things to read:

"A Story of a Monk," *De La Salle V*, page 118.
"Fasting," *Rosary Reader V*, page 238.
"Anselm and the Lizard," *American Reader V*, page 337.

12. Benedict, and the Monks

Nearly fifteen hundred years ago, a boy by the name of Benedict ran away from the Latin school in Rome and hid himself in the mountains. He was not afraid of his lessons, but of something far, far more serious. He was afraid of sin. The Roman boys with whom he went to school were not good; and Benedict knew he could not keep his heart pure if he stayed with them. Therefore he went high up into the desert mountains of Italy and lived in a cave. For three years no one knew where he was, except a hermit who brought him food. This hermit was surprised to see how the young Benedict became better and holier every day. But later others found out about the young man who lived so strict a life of prayer and penance. They came to live in the mountains near him and asked him to be the guide for their souls. Benedict built a monastery for them where each could live in a little room or cell by himself. But still others came, until he had built twelve monasteries in all, over which he acted as head or abbot. Later St. Benedict went to Monte Cassino, where he built another monastery. There he wrote a rule for his monks which is so well planned that it has been used by many monks and nuns ever since. It divides the day between prayer and work. Those who follow it carefully cannot help but become perfect.

Benedict himself knew well how to pray. Through prayer he received many favors from God. One day a man came running to the saint. In his arms he held his dead boy.

"Give me back my son," he cried.

"Such miracles are not for us to work," Benedict replied, "but for the blessed Apostles. Why do you ask me to do what my weakness cannot bear?"

But the monks joined the heart-broken father in begging for the life of the boy and at last Benedict was moved with pity.

"O Lord," he prayed, "do not look upon my sins, but upon the faith of this man, who prays for the life of his

Benedict took hold of the dead boy's hand.
The boy stood up, alive and well.

son, and give back to the body the soul which You have taken away."

The dead body began to tremble. Benedict took hold of the lifeless hand. The boy stood up, and the saint gave him back alive to his father.

When death was near, St. Benedict asked the monks to take him to the chapel. Once more he received Jesus in Holy Communion. Then, leaning on one of his monks, his hands lifted up, he died a quiet, happy death. It was the twenty-first of March in the year 543.

Now answer these questions:
1. Why did Benedict leave the Latin school?
2. Who brought him his food?
3. Why did others come to live near him?
4. Where did St. Benedict write his rule for the monks?
5. What shows that he could pray well?
6. When did St. Benedict die?

* * *

Why was Benedict afraid of sin? He knew that sin offends God and is the greatest evil in the world. He loved God and did not want to disobey or offend Him. Therefore he ran away from his bad companions. We must also be very careful with whom we go. Bad companions lead us into sin.

Do you go with bad companions? Think it over, and if you do, tell God with all your heart that you will stay away from them.

Peter goes with boys who steal. He likes the boys and says he will be very careful himself never to steal. He does not want to offend God and commit sin. What do you think about it?

Things to do:

1. The Order of St. Benedict still lives today. If you do not know how the Benedictines dress, find a picture of a Benedictine monk or nun and show it to the class.

2. St. Scholastica was the sister of St. Benedict. Read her life and tell the class about it.

3. Look up the feasts of SS. Benedict and Scholastica and find what color vestment is worn by the priest.

4. Dramatize the story of St. Benedict and the dead boy.

5. One of the saints who lived according to the rule of St. Benedict is Pope Gregory the Great who is one of the splendid lights of the Church. His feast is on March 12. Read his life and tell what he did for the Church.

Can you answer these questions?

1. What is sin?
2. Why should we avoid sin?
3. How should we avoid sin?
4. What is meant by the proximate occasion of sin?
5. When is a sin mortal?
6. When is a sin venial?
7. What happens to the soul when one commits a mortal sin?
8. What should you do if you have committed a mortal sin?
9. What is necessary for a good confession?

Good things to read:

"Marcarius the Monk," *American Cardinal Reader V*, page 129.

Test Yourself

Fifteen points make a perfect score.

1. All those in heaven, the faithful on earth, and the souls in purgatory together are called . . . .

2. The Church has its birthday on . . . . Day.

3. The number of people converted on the first Pentecost is . . . .

4. The Holy Ghost came upon the Apostles in the city of . . . .

5. Saul, the persecutor, afterwards received the name . . . .

6. The first bishop of Ephesus was . . . .

7. The Holy Bible is made up of . . . . smaller books.

8. The early Christians met in underground passages called . . . .

9. St. . . . . built up a strong Christian community in northern Africa.

10. . . . . adopted the cross as his standard and won a victory over Maxentius.

11. The creed said by the priest during Mass at certain times is called the . . . . Creed.

12. St. . . . . is called the Father of all Monks.

13. The monk who built the first monastery and wrote a famous rule for his monks is St. . . . .

14. The two Apostles who were martyred in Rome during the reign of Emperor Nero were . . . . and . . . .

UNIT IV

The Church in the Middle Ages

We know that the Apostles and their successors traveled from country to country to spread the faith of Christ. We know, too, that the Roman emperors, who ruled most of the land at that time, tried to crush Christianity and that the cross triumphed in the end. But just when it seemed that all was won and the Roman Empire would remain forever a Christian country, hordes of fierce barbarians poured in from the north and east and tore down everything that came in their way. The Roman Empire fell and with it almost all civilization. It seemed as if nothing but ruins remained.

One thing alone came through the storm unharmed. It was the Church of God, which cannot be crushed by any power on earth. And the Church, like a good mother, set to work once more, and sent her missionaries to convert the barbarian tribes. Slowly but surely the barbarians became Christians and peace and order returned. A new life and a new age began. We give that new period the name "Middle Ages." It is usually counted between the years 800 to 1500.

We shall now see the work of the Church during the Middle Ages, when she inspired her children to do great deeds and taught them to live and die for God's glory.

13. Charlemagne Becomes Emperor

It is Christmas Day in the year 800. Charlemagne, king of the Franks, has entered the basilica of St. Peter in Rome to attend Mass. As he bows down in prayer, Pope Leo III places on his head a precious crown, while all the Roman people shout: "To Charles, crowned by God, great emperor of the Romans, long life and victory!" And they burst into hymns of joy and praise.

From this time on, Charles the Great, or Charlemagne, who ruled the Roman Empire of the West, was to be the strong protector of the Church. He and the pope were to watch over the empire together for the good of the people. Charlemagne was to be the temporal head and the pope the spiritual head; that is, the emperor was to make just laws, defend the weak, and punish offenders, while the pope was to look after the spiritual good of all the citizens of the empire. Pope and emperor were to work hand in hand, although the power of each was different.

Charlemagne was not only a great conqueror and ruler but also a pious and noble Christian. From the days of his childhood he learned and practiced the Christian faith. He built a beautiful church at Aix-la-Chapelle where he went to Mass whenever it was possible.

In those days most people could not read or write.

On Christmas Day, Pope Leo III
crowns Charlemagne emperor.

Charlemagne wished to give all the people of the land a chance to learn. Therefore he founded three kinds of schools: the village schools, which were to be in charge of the parish priest; schools for singing and church music; and Cathedral schools for higher studies. The schools were to be open to all who wished to study, whether they were rich or poor.

The most famous teachers were called together from different countries to teach in the Palace School, which was the school at the palace of the emperor. There were men like Alcuin, the great Latin scholar from England, and Einhard, who later wrote the life of Charlemagne, from Germany. Others came from Italy, Ireland, and Spain. The emperor himself studied and read a great deal whenever he had time. He spoke several different languages. His favorite book was the *City of God,* which was written by St. Augustine.

Charlemagne tried to help his people and to improve his empire in every way. We can see from the rules he made that he was a wise emperor. Here are a few points that will interest you; they may seem strange to you now, but they show how many things Charlemagne thought of for the welfare of his people. The first will give you a look at the kind of food the people had in those days. The last will show you the goodness of Charlemagne's heart.

"The greatest care must be taken that whatever is prepared or made with the hands — that is, bacon, smoked meat, sausage, . . . wine, vinegar, mulberry wine, cooked wine, . . . mustard, cheese, butter, malt, beer, meal, honey, wax, flour — all should be prepared and made with the greatest cleanliness.

"Each steward on each of our domains, shall always have, for the sake of ornament, peacocks, pheasants, ducks, pigeons, partridges, and turtle-doves.

"And we command that no one in our whole kingdom shall dare to deny hospitality either to rich or poor, or to pilgrims; that is, no one shall deny shelter and fire and water to pilgrims traversing our country in God's name, or to anyone traveling for the love of God or for the safety of his own soul. If, moreover, anyone shall wish to serve them farther, let him expect the best reward from God, who Himself said: 'And who so shall receive one such little child in My name receiveth Me'; and elsewhere, 'I was a stranger, and ye took Me in.'"

After ruling his empire happily for 47 years, Charlemagne became ill in the year 814. He received Holy Viaticum and died with the words "Into Thy hands, O Lord, I commend my spirit" on his lips.

Now answer these questions:

1. When was Charlemagne crowned?
2. What was he expected to do for the Church?
3. How did Charlemagne give the people a chance for learning?
4. From what countries did teachers come to the Palace School?
5. What were the names of two of the teachers from other countries?

6. By whom was the book *City of God* written?
7. When did Charlemagne die?
8. What were his last words?

*   *   *

In the days of Charlemagne, the pope and the emperor worked hand in hand for the good of the people. We do not find the same thing today. The Church has to work almost alone and sometimes even while she is being persecuted. But it remains true just the same that a good Christian cannot be a bad citizen.

Are you a good Christian and a good citizen at the same time?

Ask yourself:

Do I often ask God to bless our country and those who rule it?

Do I obey the laws of our country and state and city because God expects me to obey them?

Do I show respect for the law and for those who represent the law?

What do you say?

Elmer is ten years old. He is not truthful, he steals when he gets a chance, he does not obey the traffic rules, and he makes fun of the police. He says some day he expects to be president of the United States. Do you think he has a good chance? Is he a good citizen? Is he a good Catholic?

Now tell about a good Catholic boy and show that he will also have to be a good citizen.

Things to do:

1. Dramatize the crowning of Charlemagne.
2. On the map find Aix-la-Chapelle.

3. Tell what you know about St. Augustine. If you do not remember his life read Lesson 8 once more.

4. Draw or cut out some of the animals that are mentioned in the rules made by Charlemagne. Write the rule made by Charlemagne next to the drawing.

5. Tell the class who else used the words which Charlemagne spoke when he was dying, and when and where it was.

6. Show in as many ways as possible how a good Catholic will be a good citizen of our country.

7. Make a list of all the qualities which you think a good citizen should have.

8. Read or recite a poem about the flag or your country.

9. Memorize the Scripture texts used in this lesson.

10. Give the salute to the flag.

11. Make a booklet illustrating the Corporal Works of Mercy.

Can you answer these questions?

1. What commandment of God tells us we must obey the rulers of our country?

2. Must the pope also obey the laws of God?

3. Must the rulers obey the laws of God?

4. Who gave the rulers or government the right to make laws?

5. Who gave the Church the right to make laws?

6. What are those works called which tell us what we must do for our neighbor's body?

7. What are the Corporal Works of Mercy?

Good things to read:

"Song of Our Lord," *Cathedral Basic Reader V*, page 215.

"What Is a Good Citizen," *Cathedral Basic Reader V*, page 216.

"George Washington," *Cathedral Basic Reader V*, page 241.

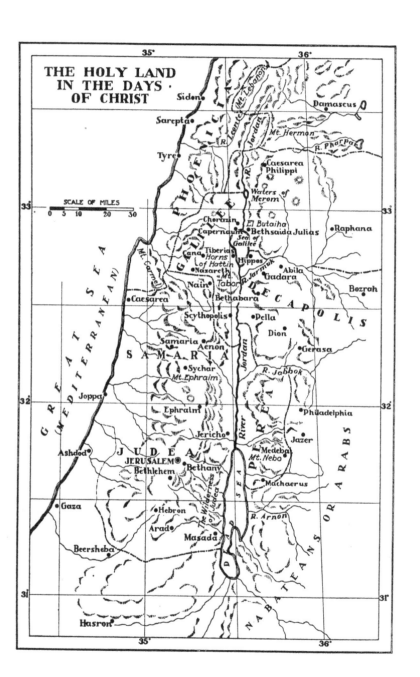

THE HOLY LAND
IN THE DAYS ·
OF CHRIST

SCALE OF MILES
0 5 10   20   30

Sidon

Sarepta

Tyre

PHOENICIA

Mt. Lebanon (Anti)

R.

R. Jordan

Damascus

Mt. Hermon

R. Pharpar

Caesarea
Philippi

Waters of
Merom

Chorazin
Capernaum
Cana
Tiberias
Horns
of Hattin
Nazareth
Nain
Caesarea

GALILEE

Mt. Carmel

El Butaiha
Bethsaida Julias
Sea of
Galilee
Hippos
Mt. Tabor
R. Jarmuk
Gadara
Abila

Raphana

Bozrah

Bethabara

Scythopolis

Pella

Dion

DECAPOLIS

Samaria   Aenon
SAMARIA
Sychar
Mt. Ephraim

Gerasa

R. Jabbok

Ephraim

Joppa

Jericho

Jordan River

Philadelphia

Jazer

P
E
R
E
A

GREAT   SEA
(MEDITERRANEAN)

Ashdod

JUDEA
JERUSALEM
Bethlehem   Bethany

Medeba
Mt. Nebo

Machaerus

Gaza

Hebron

The Wilderness of Judea

R. Arnon

Arad

Masada

DEAD SEA

Beersheba

N
A
B
A
T
E
A
N
S
    O
R
    A
R
A
B
S

Hasron

35°   36°
33°   33°
32°   32°
31°   31°
35°   36°

"Robert E. Lee: From Manliness to Manhood," *Cathedral Basic Reader V*, page 242.

"America for Me," *Catholic Youth Reader V*, page 151.

"The Flag," *Ideal Reader V*, page 194.

"Old Glory," *Rosary Reader V*, page 239.

"The Flag Was There," *Rosary Reader V*, page 244.

"Ideal Americanism," *American Reader V*, page 65.

"Roland," *American Reader V*, page 185.

14. The Holy Land Ruled by Mohammedans

When people travel through this or other countries, they usually stop at places where important things happened, or where famous people lived. It was the same with the early Christians. They loved to visit the places where Jesus lived and taught and especially where He suffered and died. And it was only right that they should do so, for the coming of the Son of God to redeem us, was the greatest of all events in the history of the world.

St. Helena, the mother of Constantine, went to Jerusalem in search of the cross on which Jesus died. After searching for a long time, she found it buried on Mt. Calvary. To show her great joy at having found this precious treasure, she built a glorious church on the spot. Every year pious pilgrims came from all parts of the world to kiss the ground on which Jesus had walked and to kneel on the spot where He had suffered and died for us.

Some time after the year 600, however, Palestine, or the Holy Land, where Jesus had lived, was captured by the Turks, who hated and persecuted the Christians. These Turks came from central Asia. Their religion was a mixture of Christian, Jewish, and pagan teachings. It was called Mohammedanism from Mohammed, who had started the religion, and who said that he was a prophet sent by God. Their religion taught them that whoever fell in battle went straight to paradise and also that no man would die until the day which was set for him by God, no matter how many arrows were shot at him. Naturally, then, these men fought gladly and fearlessly. From Asia they moved farther and farther west until they had conquered many of the countries of Europe.

With the Holy Land in the power of the Turks, we can well understand that the pilgrims who went to visit the holy places were not kindly treated. Some were killed, others returned with stories of robbery, torture, and other cruelties.

The hearts of the Christians were sad at the thought that the land which was dearest to them on earth should be in the hands of the cruel Turks. They hoped and prayed that some day God would help them overcome their enemy and once more deliver the Holy Land into Christian hands. How, after many years of sorrow and suffering, chivalrous knights went out to fight the Turks is told in the story of the great Crusades which started in the year 1096.

Now answer these questions:

1. What was the greatest of all events in the history of the world?

2. Why did the Christians visit the holy places where Jesus lived and died?

3. What did St. Helena look for in Jerusalem?

4. What did she do to show her great joy?

5. By what other name is the Holy Land called?

6. Who captured Palestine?

7. What did Mohammed say of himself?

8. Why did the Mohammedans go to battle gladly and fearlessly?

9. What happened to the pilgrims that went to Palestine?

* * *

St. Helena, the mother of Emperor Constantine, was filled with joy when she found the true cross. To show how much she honored the place where the cross was buried, she built a beautiful temple on the spot.

Have you ever seen a part of the true cross? Have you seen other relics? The Church wants us to honor the bodies of her saints and other relics because they remind us of the saints and make us want to imitate them.

Things to do:

1. If you have ever visited a place of historical interest tell the class about it.

2. Read once more the story of the conversion of Constantine.

3. Read the life of St. Helena and tell the class how she discovered the true cross.

4. On the map find Palestine, Jerusalem, Asia.

5. Find out whether there are relics of saints in your church and whose relics they are.

6. When we make the Stations of the Cross we visit in spirit the places where our Lord made His last journey and suffered for our sins. Can you make the Stations of the Cross? Make them today for the conversion of sinners.

Can you answer these questions?

1. Why did Christ suffer and die for us?
2. Why do Catholics honor the relics of the saints?
3. Do all people go straight to heaven when they die?
4. Where do those go who die with mortal sin on their souls? With venial sin?
5. May we expose ourselves to danger and say that God will protect us?
6. What do we call the sin by which we expect God's help without making the use of the proper means?
7. What are we commanded by the fifth commandment?

Good things to read:

"The Stations of the Cross," *The Catholic Youth Reader VI,* page 437.

15. God Wills It

An immense crowd was gathered in the city of Clermont. Pope Urban II himself had come to France to speak to the people, and all were eager to hear and see him. And such a sermon as the pope preached that day! His heart was full of sorrow. He had heard so much about the Turks in the Holy Land that he could no longer restrain himself. We can almost see him standing there above the crowd and hear his fiery words!

"O Christians, Christians! Can you bear the thought that the cross is being trampled under foot in the holiest city on earth? Can you bear to see Mohammed, the false prophet, honored in the very spot where Christ was buried? The Church of the Ascension — oh, that we could kiss the ground on which it stands — has become a stable for horses and camels. Our Christian pilgrims are robbed, insulted, killed. Many are not allowed to enter the city after they have traveled hundreds of miles and suffered hunger, cold, and many other hardships. Christians! There are millions of you here in Europe. There are hundreds of thousands of noble knights, from Spain to Sweden, and from England to Poland. How can you show your courage and your love of God better than by fighting for the Holy Land? Fear nothing! the Church will take care of you and your families. Forward, then, if you have any love for Christ, if you have any courage and honor! Forward to Jerusalem! Fight and win! God wills it!"

For a moment everything must have been as silent as the grave. Then, from a hundred thousand throats rang out the cry: "God wills it!" And the words echoed again from all the Christian countries. Soon brave knights came riding from every side with shining armor and flying banners, ready to give their lives for Christ and the Holy Land.

All those who wished to join in the war against the

The crusaders pause in prayer outside
the walls of Jerusalem.

Turks, were given a cross of cloth to wear on their right shoulder. All who wore the cross are called crusaders and the wars in which they fought are known as the Crusades.

It was a glorious beginning. But the hardships were so many and so great that thousands lost their lives, before they ever reached Jerusalem. At last, after terrible bloodshed, the city was taken by the crusaders. They made their leader, Godfrey of Bouillon, king. He refused to wear the crown, however, for he said he could not wear a crown of gold in the place where Christ had worn a crown of thorns.

The Christians held Jerusalem for almost a century. But the Turks surrounded them on all sides and gave them no peace. Help for the crusaders was far away and long in coming; and so, after 88 years, the Holy City fell again into Turkish hands.

Again and again the popes called upon the people in the west to free the Holy Land from Turkish rule, and again and again brave knights went over land and sea to fight under the banner of the cross. One time about 50,000 children formed a crusade and went singing and praying through the streets. They hoped to deliver Jerusalem by their prayers and hymns. But many died on the way and many others were sold to the Mohammedans as slaves. Very few ever came back to their parents. This is known as the Children's Crusade.

Eight different times great crusades were undertaken

under different leaders; but Palestine never remained under Christian rule for long. Yet, in spite of failure, much good came out of these wars. In the first place they united the Christian nations more closely and stopped the Mohammedans from destroying Christian countries. The crusaders also learned a great many things in science, literature, and art from the Turks and brought this new learning back to their own countries. Finally, the crusades gave us the Orders of Christian Knights. They stood for faith, respect for virtue, and charity to the poor and needy. A great change soon came over Europe as a result of the crusades. Explorations and inventions followed quickly and brought new lands and new ideas into the lives of the people.

Now answer these questions:

1. Which pope went to Clermont to preach to the people?
2. What did he tell them to do?
3. How did the people answer?
4. Why were the men who went to the war called crusaders?
5. What were the wars called?
6. Who was the leader of the crusaders?
7. Why would he not wear a crown of gold?
8. Did the Christians keep Jerusalem?
9. How did the children hope to win the war?
10. Did they succeed?
11. What good results did the crusades have?

* * *

Boys and girls of today cannot join in a crusade like that of the knights of long ago, but they can still work for Christ and do just as much good as the crusaders. Do you want to be a crusader for Christ? Here are some ways in which you can fight for Christ:

Tell Christ often that you want Him for your Leader.

Learn from Him how to speak and act.

Do not allow yourself any words or actions which your great Leader would not like.

Do not let others speak against Him or use His name lightly.

Salute your Leader often in the Blessed Sacrament, and tell Him you love Him.

Things to do:

1. On the map find Clermont in France.

2. The crusaders went to Jerusalem by way of Constantinople. Suppose they started in France or Germany, what direction would they have traveled?

3. Find pictures of crusaders and knights and bring them to school to show to the class.

4. Imagine that you are one of the children living during the time of the crusades. Write a letter to your friend in another city, telling her all about the Children's Crusade which you are going to join in a few days. Tell her where you expect to go and what you plan to do.

5. Make or draw a knight's shield or banner with the cross and the words "God Wills It" on it.

6. Find a picture of Sir Galahad and read the poem "Sir Galahad" by Tennyson. Memorize the two lines which begin "My strength is as the strength of ten."

7. There are many beautiful stories written about knights. Read one of them and tell the class about it.

Can you answer these questions?

1. What do we mean when we say that all should do the will of God?

2. Does God take care of us?

3. Then why is there so much evil in the world?

4. Whom has God given to each one of us for our special protection?

5. What do the angels do for us?

6. Who made the angels?

7. Did they all remain good?

8. What are the bad angels called?

9. How do they try to harm us?

Good things to read:

"By Degrees," *Ideal Reader V*, page 108.

"St. George of Cappadocia," *Misericordia Reader V*, page 379.

"How Sir Lancelot Saved the Queen," *Misericordia Reader V*, page 391.

"What It Meant to Be a Knight," *American Reader V*, page 176.

16. Louis, King and Saint

Queen Blanche of Castile was telling her little son Louis about God. The Little Prince loved nothing better than to sit at her knee and listen to her words.

"My son," she was saying to him, "I love you very, very much. But I would rather see you dead at my feet than ever have you commit a mortal sin."

Prince Louis never forgot those words. "What a terrible thing it must be to offend God," he thought to himself. "I will never, never commit a mortal sin."

When he was only seven years old, he became king of France. What do you think he made up his mind to do?

"I am going to defend the honor of God. I am going to protect the poor and the weak. I am going to crush heresy and unbelief." These are some of the wonderful things King Louis decided to do. But he did not only make up his mind to do great and noble deeds, he started at once to put his desires into action. He made wise laws, built beautiful temples for the glory of God, and helped the pope to carry out the laws of the Church.

In the year 1245 Pope Innocent IV called on the Christian world to undertake another crusade for the delivery of Jerusalem from the Turks. Louis, the fearless King, answered the call at once. He gathered the bravest knights of France around him and set out for Cairo, Egypt, where the ruler of Jerusalem lived at that time. But there he was defeated and taken prisoner with his men.

If Louis was the first, the best, and the bravest of Christian soldiers in France, he showed himself even more a true knight in captivity. At one time a Mohammedan prince came rushing into his tent, and threatened to stab him unless he made a knight of him. "No unbeliever can perform the duties of a Christian knight," Louis answered calmly.

At another time he was told that he could have his liberty if he would take an oath. Louis felt that the words he was to use would offend God. With their swords pointed at his throat, the unbelievers tried to force him to pronounce the oath. He refused. They threatened to massacre the Christians. Louis still refused. He must have been thinking of the words which

St. Louis, King of France.

his holy mother Blanche spoke to him, when, as a little boy, he sat at her knee, while she told him about the goodness of God and the wickedness of sin.

At last a ransom was paid for Louis and his soldiers,

and he was allowed to go free. After visiting Palestine, he went home and ruled his people as wisely as before. But the heart of the great king was not satisfied. Jerusalem was still in the power of the Turks.

Once more he and his chivalrous knights set out with hearts on fire for the cause of God. This time they would surely set the Holy City free. They landed in Tunis, Africa, and won a victory over the enemy. Before they could go on, however, a deadly fever broke out in the camp and Louis himself became a victim. When he was dying, he knelt beside his bed and received the Viaticum. Then he gave up his pure soul to God. It did not matter that he had not reached Jerusalem. He had been a faithful Christian knight; he was ready to enter the great Kingdom, and to serve forever the King of kings.

Now answer these questions:

1. Who was the mother of King Louis?
2. What did she tell her little boy?
3. How old was Louis when he became king?
4. What did Louis do for his people?
5. Why did Louis undertake a crusade?
6. What happened to him in Cairo?
7. Why would he not take the oath that would have set him free?
8. How did Louis and his men get their freedom?
9. Why was the heart of the king not satisfied after he came home?
10. Did he and his men reach Jerusalem when they set out the second time?
11. In what country did St. Louis die?

*   *   *

Louis was a fearless knight. He had made up his mind that he would never offend God by committing mortal sin. He knew how to say "No," even when it might have cost him his life. Can you say "No" when you are tempted or asked to do wrong, even if it is in smaller things? If you can overcome yourself in little things, you will learn to overcome yourself in great temptations also.

Ask yourself:

Can you say "No"?

You have not studied your lessons. Your friend calls you to come out and play with him.

Mother asks you to run an errand. You want to go on reading an interesting story.

Jack tells you about a place where the boys get plenty of oranges without being caught. He offers to take you along.

You are out on a hike with a group of boys. It is Friday. They all eat wieners and ask you to eat some too. You are very hungry.

You are in a store. A lady just dropped a dollar bill. She did not notice it and is walking out. You pick it up. You want to keep it.

The boys of your team break a big window. They cannot afford to pay for it. They plan to deny that they did it.

Mrs. Lee is leaving the city for the day. She gives you 50 cents to stay around the house until evening. There is a good movie in the afternoon, and you want to see it. Mrs. Lee will never know the difference.

You have committed a sin of which you are very much ashamed. You are tempted not to mention it in confession.

Are you sure that you can say "No" when you are tempted?

Watch yourself today and see whether you can be a brave knight like St. Louis.

Things to do:

1. Dramatize a scene from the life of St. Louis.

2. On the map of Africa find Cairo in Egypt, and Tunis in Algeria. Show the route which crusaders had to take and tell what sea they had to cross.

3. Write a little play about a boy or girl who defended the honor of God.

4. Imagine that you lived in France at the time of King Louis. Write a letter to a friend telling about one of the king's noble deeds.

5. Draw the banner you think St. Louis used in the crusades.

6. Learn the hymn "To Christ the King."

Can you answer these questions?

1. What is necessary to make a sin mortal?

2. May you commit a mortal sin to save your life?

3. Is it right to say a sin is only venial and therefore not so bad?

4. What happens when a person is not careful about committing venial sins?

5. What should a person do who has committed a mortal sin?

Good things to read:

"My Mother," *Ideal Reader V*, page 44.

"Dare to Do Right," *Ideal Reader V*, page 246.

"St. Louis," *Misericordia Reader V*, page 26.

"The Fearless Saint," *A Child's Garden of Religious Stories*, page 231.

Test Yourself

A Game with the Saints

Not all of the answers to these questions are in your book, but you will have fun finding them elsewhere. Ask each other these questions and see whether you can score 25 points.

1. The greatest saint in heaven.
2. The saint who is pictured with keys in his hand.
3. The Apostle of the Gentiles.
4. The Apostle who has a cross named after him.
5. A saintly queen who preferred to see her son dead rather than have him commit a mortal sin.
6. The patroness of sacred music.
7. The Apostle who stood beneath the cross.
8. The saint who baptized Jesus on the Jordan.
9. The mother of the Blessed Virgin.
10. The saint who offered a veil to Jesus to wipe His face on the way to Calvary.
11. The doubting Apostle.
12. The saint who discovered the true cross.
13. The patron of the whole Catholic Church.
14. The saint whose son also became a saint through her many prayers.
15. The first martyr.
16. The father of the Blessed Virgin.
17. The hermit who became the Father of Monks.
18. The saint who wrote a famous rule for his Order.
19. The girl saint who is pictured with a lamb on her arm.
20. The saint who washed the feet of our Lord with her tears.
21. The patron against diseases of the throat.

22. The saint who is pictured with a heart in his hand.
23. The saintly king who led a crusade.
24. The saint to whom St. Paul wrote two epistles.
25. The Apostle who took the place of the traitor Judas.

UNIT V

Great Popes of the Middle Ages

Sad times had come for the Church of the Middle Ages. Wickedness seemed to rise up on every side. The rulers did not always follow the example of the great Christian Emperor Charlemagne. Instead of helping and protecting the pope, some of them went so far as to take the government of the Church into their own hands. Even the popes were sometimes weak and unworthy. It looked as if the Master Himself were sleeping. "Lord, save us!" the faithful must have prayed, for they feared that the Church would perish.

But Christ was not asleep. During these troubled times He sent two great popes to lead His Church safely through the terrible storms that arose on all sides. These two popes were Gregory VII, also called Hildebrand, who reigned from 1073 to 1085; and Innocent III, known as the "Tamer of Kings," who occupied the Chair of St. Peter from 1198 to 1216.

17. Gregory VII

In the year 1020 a little boy was born of poor parents in Tuscany, Italy. The boy's name was Hildebrand. He was chosen by God to be a great defender of the rights of the Church at a time when kings and princes were trying their best to rule the Church and even to take charge of her spiritual affairs.

When Hildebrand was still young, his uncle took him to Rome and had him educated in the school of the Lateran Palace. How happy the boy was, to be in the great city of Rome. He studied hard and learned to love the Eternal City with all his heart.

When Hildebrand was older, he became the pope's secretary. Soon the young man learned that the Church was going through evil days. Kings and princes were selfish and unjust. They oppressed the people, mistreated bishops and even the pope, if he did not do their will. Sometimes things looked so dark and troubled that it seemed as if the whole world had become bad.

The pope was later banished from Rome and Hildebrand followed him. After the pope's death, Hildebrand went to France to the famous Benedictine monastery of Cluny. This monastery was a renowned center of learning, where many splendid leaders and great saints received their training. It was at Cluny that the next pope,

97

Leo IX, found Hildebrand. Leo took him back to Rome, where for 23 years he stood by the popes one after the other and helped them in fighting the evils that threatened the Church on all sides.

At last Hildebrand himself was elected pope. He was called Gregory VII. No one knew better than he what it meant to guide the Church in those terrible times. To be at the head of the Church at that time meant to fight against powerful kings and princes, who claimed the right to appoint bishops and priests to their office and who even went so far as to imprison a pope if he did not do their will. To be pope meant to have many bitter enemies and few trusted friends; it meant to stand almost alone in the fight for the rights of the Church.

But Gregory knew that he did not stand alone. There was One with him who was stronger than all the powerful princes of the earth; and that was Christ Himself, who had promised the Apostles: "Behold, I am with you all days even to the consummation of the world."

Gregory began at once to make war on all who were guilty of wrong, whether they were kings, princes, bishops, or priests. There were especially three great evils that he had to fight. The first was simony, or the selling of holy offices. No one but the Church can say who is worthy to be a bishop or to hold any other high office of the Church. Yet many rulers claimed this right and accepted large sums of money in return. The second evil was the conduct of the unworthy bishops and priests who refused to obey the strict laws which had been made by the pope for the good of the Church; and the third was the claim of kings and princes that they had the right to appoint new bishops. It was a tremendous task to fight against all these evils, and it took a man who had made himself strong by prayer and self-denial to carry out the work to the end.

Perhaps the greatest trouble of all was made by King Henry IV of Germany. In spite of the pope's orders that kings must not appoint bishops, Henry continued to do so. Gregory excommunicated him. When Henry saw that the pope's power was stronger than his, he went to the castle of Canossa to kneel at the pope's feet and to tell him he was sorry for his disobedience. For three days Henry did public penance, by standing barefoot in the snow before the castle. Gregory thought that King Henry was really sorry for his sins, and gave him absolution. But soon the king showed that he was not sincere. He was hardly gone, when he continued to break the laws of God and of the Church as before. Then he was once more excommunicated by the pope. Henry sent his troops against Rome and the pope had to leave the city. He died shortly afterward. He had loved justice and hated evil, as he himself said, and therefore he had to die in exile.

Although Gregory died before the struggle for the rights of the Church was over, the victory was really won by him. In the twelve short years that he was pope, he had shown that the Church is more powerful than kings and must be obeyed in spiritual matters even by the rulers of the world.

He is honored by the Church as a saint of God and as one of the greatest popes of all times.

Now answer these questions:
1. Where was Hildebrand educated?
2. What did Hildebrand soon learn in Rome?
3. Where did he go after the pope's death?
4. Where did Pope Leo IX take him?
5. How long did he help the popes?
6. What was Hildebrand called after he was elected pope?
7. Did Gregory stand alone in his fight against evil?
8. Who made the greatest trouble of all?
9. How did Henry do penance?
10. Was he sincere?
11. How long was Gregory VII pope?
12. What did he do for the church during that time?

* * *

St. Gregory VII was willing to suffer everything rather than to give in to evil. He was a strong character, otherwise he would never have been able to stand as firmly as he did. You will also be called upon sometimes to be a champion for the rights of the Church. But in order to be strong enough, you must be prepared. Read the life of St. Gregory once more and find how he became strong to carry on the war against evil.

There is much evil in the world also today. What can you do to help fight it?

Ask yourself:

Do I know my religion so well that I can defend it before others?

Do I keep the laws of God and the Church myself?

Do I allow others to say things against God and the Church?

Do I give a bad example to my little sisters and brothers?

Study the Scripture text: "He said therefore to them again: Peace be to you. As the Father hath sent Me, I also send you. When He had said this, He breathed on them: and He said to them: Receive ye the Holy Ghost. Whose sins you shall forgive, they are forgiven them: and whose sins you shall retain, they are retained."

Can you answer these questions?

1. Who is the visible head of the Church?
2. Who made him the visible ruler?
3. Which sacrament does the Scripture text speak about?
4. How must our contrition be in order to have our sins forgiven?
5. What was missing in Henry's contrition?
6. What sins must we confess?
7. What else must we do when we go to confession besides being sorry for sin?
8. What does it mean to be excommunicated?
9. What is simony?
10. How can simony be practiced today?

Good things to read:

"A Builder's Lesson," *De La Salle Reader V*, page 235.

"Charles Carrol of Carrolton," *Catholic Youth Reader V*, page 375.

"Don Looks Ahead," *American Cardinal V*, page 225.

18. Innocent III

In the Vatican garden the pope was about to receive a visitor. As he looked up, his face showed surprise. The stranger was dressed in a poor brown garment, with a rope tied around his waist. His hair and beard were long. He looked like a beggar. The pope did not seem pleased and soon the stranger was gone again.

That night the pope had a dream. He saw the walls of the Lateran Church, the first of all churches in Rome, on the point of tumbling down. Then a man came and held the church up and made it strong again. The man was dressed in a poor brown garment, with a rope around his waist, his hair and beard long; he looked like a beggar. The next morning the pope sent for the stranger who had visited him in the Vatican garden and gave him the permission for which he had asked. He saw that the man was a saint.

The stranger was the Little Poor Man of Assisi, St. Francis, and the pope was Innocent III, whose labors for the Church were so many and so great.

Nearly one hundred years after Pope St. Gregory had died, it looked once more as if the Church would soon lose all temporal power, and the emperors would rule both the Church and the State. Then Innocent III was elected as head of the Church. He was the son of a noble family in Italy and received his early training in Rome. He was still a young man when he became pope. Firmly

Pope Innocent III blesses St. Francis of Assisi
and approves his plans to found his Order.

and fearlessly he faced his duty. Kings and princes had taken much land from the popes in the past. He protested against the wrong, strengthened the rights of the Church and in one year made the rulers give back what they had taken.

He made peace between kings and princes and called upon them to join in a great crusade to drive the Turks from the Holy Land. The crusaders started out but fought in other places and failed to reach the Holy Land. Innocent was disappointed; for like the other popes before him, he desired with all his heart, to free the Holy Land from Turkish rule.

The Turks were called Moors in the West. For a long time they had been moving farther and farther into the Christian countries. While they were crossing the Strait of Gibraltar, trying to get into Spain, the Christian rulers were fighting among themselves. It was Innocent, the Pope, who saw the danger, forced the quarreling rulers to make peace with one another and unite for battle against the Moors. He himself sent them help and encouragement and offered up public prayers for their success. The result was a glorious victory for the Christians in July, 1212.

Pope Innocent also wrote a number of books and approved two great Orders, the Order of St. Francis and the Order of St. Dominic, about which we shall hear more later. Both of these orders were great helps to him in spreading the faith and making the Church firm and strong. He also built a large hospital in Rome called

"Santo Spiritu." It was the largest hospital of its kind and served as a model for our hospitals of today.

The last great work of Pope Innocent III was to call a General Council in Rome in 1215. It was called the Lateran Council and was the most brilliant meeting that had been seen since the Council of Nicæa. There were about 1,300 cardinals, archbishops, bishops, and priests present from every land in Europe and the East. Many important questions were talked over. There was need of men and money for another crusade. The Church had to make some of her teachings more clear and had to condemn a heresy which was spreading over Europe. It also made the law that Holy Communion must be received at least once a year.

This great Council was a fitting close to the life of Pope Innocent. He died eight months later. He had seen the many dangers that threatened the Church; he had made her temporal power strong; and, like the great leader that he was, he had dealt firmly and wisely with rulers and kings for the good of the whole Christian world.

Now answer these questions:
1. How did the stranger look who came to see the pope?
2. What dream did the pope have?
3. Who was the poor man?
4. Who was the pope?
5. What did the pope call on the princes to do?
6. Did they succeed?
7. What were the Turks called in the West?

8. What was happening while the Christian rulers were fighting among themselves?

9. How did the pope show himself a great leader during this time?

10. What building did the pope put up in Rome?

11. What was the last work of Innocent III?

* * *

Innocent III was very young when he was elected pope. His duties were many and hard. He faced them fearlessly and saved the Church from the power of selfish rulers. Your duties are not yet so great, but it takes a strong will to do even small duties well.

Do you do your duty?

Toward God by obeying His Commandments?

Toward the Church by being a good parishioner?

Toward your parents by being obedient and loving children?

Toward your teachers by studying your lessons every day?

Toward others by doing to them as you would wish them to do to you?

Toward yourselves by trying to become better children of God and better citizens of your country every day?

Talk these duties over. See whether there are some you have not been careful about. Make up your mind to do one thing well today. Tonight when you examine your conscience ask yourself whether you have kept your resolution. If you have, tell God how glad you are and thank Him for His help; if not, tell God that you are sorry and try again tomorrow.

Can you answer these questions?

1. What commandments tell us our duty toward God?

2. What commandment of the Church tells us our duty toward our pastor and parish?

3. What commandment tells us we must receive Holy Communion at least once a year?
4. How often should we receive Holy Communion?
5. What is necessary to receive Holy Communion worthily?
6. How should one act when receiving Holy Communion?
7. Who gave the Church the right to make laws?
8. Who said "Blessed are the peacemakers"?
9. Where are these words to be found?
10. How can you be a peacemaker?

Good things to read:

"The Soldier's Reprieve," *Misericordia Reader V*, page 122.
"Ruth," *American Reader V*, page 46.
"The Leak in the Dike," *Misericordia Reader V*, page 356.

Can You Find Them?

The following sentences are all taken from Holy Scripture. Look for them in the Holy Bible and tell something about the story. Numbers 2 and 4 are taken from epistles. Tell to whom and by whom they were written.

1. "If thou wilt be perfect, go sell what thou hast, and give to the poor, and thou shalt have treasure in heaven, and come, follow Me" (Matt. xix. 21).
2. "Without faith it is impossible to please God" (Heb. xi. 6).
3. "He that heareth you, heareth Me; and he that despiseth you, despiseth Me; and he that despiseth Me, despiseth Him that sent Me" (Luke x. 16).
4. "There are three who give testimony in heaven, the Father, the Word, and the Holy Ghost. And these three are one" (I John v. 7).

5. "Thomas answered and said to Him: My Lord and my God" (John xx. 28).

6. "All power is given to Me in heaven and in earth" (Matt. xxviii. 18).

7. "And suddenly there came a sound from heaven, as of a mighty wind coming, and it filled the whole house where they were sitting."

8. "And there appeared to them parted tongues as it were of fire, and it sat upon every one of them, and they were all filled with the Holy Ghost" (Acts ii. 2–4).

9. "If thou wilt enter into life, keep the commandments" (Matt. xix. 17).

10. "For what doth it profit a man, if he gain the whole world, and suffer the loss of his own soul" (Matt. xvi. 26).

UNIT VI

Great Saints of the Middle Ages

We have read of the sad times which had come for Church and State during the Middle Ages. The monasteries, we remember, were built far away from cities and the monks prayed and worked mostly by themselves. Times were changing, however, and the Church needed more men who would go out and preach to the people. The Holy Land was again in the hands of the Turks; Christian countries, kings and princes were disobedient to the Church; men were often proud, unjust, and cruel. It was then that God called up the two great popes whose lives we have read, and a number of other saints to help the Church in her greatest need.

We shall now hear about St. Bernard, St. Francis, St. Dominic, and St. Thomas Aquinas, some of the greatest saints of the Middle Ages. These men helped the popes in fighting against the evils of the times.

19. St. Bernard

In the castle of Fontaine, in France, there was great disturbance and sadness. Bernard, the most promising member of the family, was going to enter a monastery. Not only was he going to be a monk, but he was going to join the Cistercian Order, from which most men were staying away, because it was the strictest and poorest of them all. His family and friends felt that they must do their best to stop him. They must show him that he was all wrong.

Bernard listened to them. When they had finished, he began to speak. He told them what it meant to follow Christ. He told them that he would receive a hundred-fold, for all that he left. He told them how much nobler it was to be poor than rich, to be humble than proud. At last they understood; and when he was preparing to leave, four of his brothers, his uncle, and many of his friends were ready to go with him.

When Bernard and his companions said good-by to the youngest son, who was to stay with his father, they said to him:

"Now you will be heir to everything."

"Yes," he answered, "you leave the earth to me, and keep heaven for yourselves. Do you call that fair?" And he, too, left all to become a monk.

At last the old father himself left wealth and honor and became a poor monk with his son.

In the monastery at Citeaux, Bernard prayed and

It was the monk, St. Bernard,
who preached the second
crusade.

worked hand in hand with the others; but most of all he tried to become a perfect monk. Before long so many came to join him, that it was necessary to build a new monastery. The fame of Bernard, who was leading the life of a saint, spread over the country, and soon the sick were brought from far and wide to be healed by his touch and his prayers. In less than forty years seventy monasteries had been built in all parts of Europe as branches of the house to which St. Bernard belonged.

But St. Bernard was called by God to even greater work. Popes, bishops, and kings asked him for his help. He made peace between cities, between kings and their people, even between the rulers in the Church itself. It was the time after the first crusade. Jerusalem was again threatened by the Turks. Pope Eugene III called on him to preach a second crusade. Bernard went from place to place and preached in words that seemed on fire with love for God and the Holy Land. "The Cross! the Cross!" men shouted throughout France; and they came to the saint to have a cloth cross fastened on their shoulders. At last, when there was no more cloth left, Bernard took his own cloak and cut it to pieces to make more crosses.

From France St. Bernard went to Germany. In the cathedral at Speyer the crowd was so great that he could not get through to the altar. Then Emperor Conrad III took him up on his shoulders and carried him to the sanctuary. Here his sermon so touched the emperor that he, also, took the cross and joined the crusade.

At last Bernard returned to his monastery worn out by his penance and labors. He died in the year 1153. The pope gave him the title of honor "Doctor of the Church."

Now answer these questions:

1. Why did Bernard's family want to stop him from becoming a monk?
2. Did they succeed?
3. Who went with Bernard?
4. What kind of life did Bernard live in the monastery?
5. What did the pope ask him to do?
6. What happened when Bernard preached the crusade in France?
7. Why could he not get through the cathedral in Speyer?
8. Who helped him to get to the sanctuary?
9. What title of honor did the Church give Bernard?

* * *

St. Bernard spoke so beautifully about the vocation of a monk that many followed him into the convent. Do you know anything about convent life? Ask your teacher to tell you more about it. Perhaps God will not call you to leave your home and follow Him more closely. It will be well for you, however, to know just what the religious or convent life means. Many people do not understand it, and believe foolish stories about monks and nuns. As a good child of the Church, you should be able to tell them of the great work that has been done by these men and women in the past and all that is still being done by them.

Pray often to God to find out what kind of work He wants you to do in life.

Things to do:

1. Find pictures of different monks and nuns. Can you tell to which Order they belong?
2. If you have religious teachers, find out to which Order they belong and who founded it.
3. Dramatize parts of the story you have just read.

4. Find when the Feast of St. Bernard is celebrated.

5. The prayer *Memorare* is called St. Bernard's prayer. If you do not know it, look for it in your prayer book and learn it by heart.

6. Learn the hymn "Remember, Holy Mary" (*Gregory Hymnal*) which has the same thoughts as the prayer.

7. Find the story of the rich young man and tell the class about it. Memorize the words: "If thou wilt be perfect, go sell what thou hast, and give to the poor, and thou shalt have treasure in heaven: and come follow Me" (Matt. xix. 21). Where have you read some of these words before?

8. The cathedral of Speyer is one of the most beautiful in the world. See what you can learn about this great cathedral. If you can find a picture of it, show it to the class.

9. Tell all the different kinds of vocations you know: doctor, nurse, priest, etc.

10. Write the names of other Doctors of the Church whom you have learned about and the year of each one's death.

Can you answer these questions?

1. What do you mean by a vocation? A religious vocation? What is your father's vocation?

2. Was it right for Bernard's friends to try to keep him from following his vocation?

3. Religious usually take vows. Do you know what a vow is?

4. May anyone take a vow?

5. May one break a vow?

Good things to read:

"The Youth of the Holy Priest of Ars," *American Cardinal Reader V*, page 156.

"St. Aloysius," *Catholic Youth VI*, page 80.

"A Brave Rescue," *Catholic Youth VI*, page 289.

"Opportunity," *Catholic Youth VI*, page 185.

JESUS THE VERY THOUGHT OF THEE

St. Bernard

Jesus, the very thought of Thee,
  With sweetness fills my breast;
But sweeter far Thy Face to see
  And in Thy presence rest.

Nor voice can sing, nor heart can frame,
  Nor can the mem'ry find
A sweeter sound than Thy blest Name,
  O Savior of mankind!

O Hope of every contrite Heart,
  O Joy of all the meek.
To those who fall, how kind Thou art,
  How good to those who seek.

Jesus, our only joy be Thou,
  As Thou our prize wilt be;
O Jesus, be our glory now
  And through eternity.

20. The Little Poor Man of Assisi

We remember how the first hermits left everything
they had and became poor for the love of God. Even
when later the monks lived together under one roof,
they remained very poor and earned their daily bread

by the work of their hands. By and by, however, some of the convents began to own land and to gather wealth. Some of the monks no longer lived the strict lives of the early hermits and were not a good example to the people.

One day a wealthy young man of Assisi, dressed in a rough brown garment, with a rope tied about the waist, appeared in the streets of the town. The people of Assisi who, like most people of those days, were fond of riches and fine clothes, could not understand what had happened.

"Why does Francis, the son of the rich cloth merchant, wear such miserable clothes?" they asked one another.

Soon they learned the truth. Francis had been very ill. When he recovered, he was a changed man. He saw how foolish it was to put fine clothing on the body and forget the care of the soul. He saw, too, that if men wanted to convert others to Christ, they themselves would first have to become poor and humble, like Christ, their Leader. Love of wealth was the great disease of the age. It would have to be cured by the opposite virtue, love of poverty.

And that is how it happened that one day Francis took off his rich garments in the presence of his father, and chose poverty as his companion and friend.

Soon other young men joined him and together they formed a new company of monks known as the Franciscan Order. They had nothing of their own, living only on the alms that were given to them by others.

The new Order spread rapidly. The monks went from country to country and preached to the people. They were helping the pope to make the Church, which seemed to be on the point of ruin, strong and firm once more. And because they were poor and their own hearts were filled with a burning love for God, they brought many souls back to Christ.

Francis himself, by his great love for God and the poor, became one of the greatest saints of the Church. His love reached out not only to men but to all of God's creatures. Even animals seemed to know how much he cared for them, for they would gather around him while he prayed and would listen to him when he spoke about God's love for them. He called the animals, and even the sun and moon and stars, his brothers and sisters and asked them all to help him praise the Lord. What a beautiful soul Francis must have had!

One time, during the crusades, Francis went to the Holy Land. He hoped to become a martyr there, for the sultan had put a price on every Christian head. Francis even went so far as to preach before the sultan.

"I will go through fire for the Christian faith," Francis told him.

The sultan was surprised at the courage of the saint and let him go unharmed.

At another time Francis said to one of the monks:

"Come, let us go out and preach."

Together they walked around the town, simple, humble, silent, and then returned to their convent.

"But, Father Francis," said the astonished monk, "did you not say we were going to preach?"

"And don't you think we preached a better sermon by our good example," asked Francis, "than by many words?"

Is it surprising that thousands of people came to this wonderful saint and asked to join his Order? Even women wished to serve God in the Order of St. Francis. Therefore, together with St. Clare, he founded a convent for women, so that they, too, might live for God alone. But still others came, married men and women among them, asking Francis to receive them into the Franciscan Order. The saint knew that God needed good men and women in the world also. Therefore he started the "Third Order of St. Francis" to which all people may belong who wish to lead more perfect lives but cannot enter a convent. Many men and women around us belong to this Order, although we may not know about it. They have special prayers and rules, but they remain at home or go to work just as people usually do.

The last year of St. Francis' life had come. He was kneeling alone in prayer with his arms stretched out in the form of a cross. Then a wonderful thing happened. Jesus on the cross appeared to him and gave him the marks of His five wounds. It was a sign of the great love which God had for this little poor man of Assisi.

Francis died shortly afterward, in the year 1226, with the words on his lips: "Welcome, sister Death."

He was poor on earth. In heaven he found riches far greater than the world can give.

Now answer these questions:

1. How was Francis of Assisi dressed?
2. Why did he give up his wealth?
3. How did the Franciscan monks get food and clothing?
4. How did the animals act toward Francis?
5. Why did Francis go to the Holy Land?
6. How did Francis preach a sermon in the town?
7. What two other Orders did he found?
8. Who may belong to the "Third Order of St. Francis"?
9. How did Francis hope to become a martyr?
10. What happened to him the last year of his life?
11. What were his last words?

* * *

Did you ever hear the saying "Actions speak louder than words"? What do the words mean? How did St. Francis show that he understood these words?

Did you ever stop to think that you also preach by your actions every day? Here are a few ways by which your actions help others or keep others from doing right. See how many more you can add to the list:

1. You and your little brother are sent upstairs to say night prayers and go to bed. You do not say your prayers but go right to bed. Your little brother watches you and then does the same. What do your actions show?

2. Sister gives you some problems to work in school. You copy from your neighbor. Mary sees you and also copies.

3. During Lent you get up early every morning and go to Mass. Your friend hears about it and wants to go with you.

4. You and the neighbor's boy are walking along the street.

A case of apples drops from a delivery wagon. You call the driver and help him pick up the apples. The boy with you thinks you are foolish, but he follows your example.

5. You are out camping with some boys. On Sunday morning you tell the boys you are going to hike to the nearest church for Mass. They did not intend to go; but now two of the boys say they will go along.

6. A little lame dog is running through the alley. You pick up stones to throw at him. Soon there are more boys throwing stones at the dog.

Things to do:

1. Tell what you remember of the two hermits that you have read about in your book.

2. If you know any Franciscan priests or Sisters tell the class how they are dressed or show pictures of them.

3. There are many beautiful stories and poems written about St. Francis of Assisi. Read one and tell it to the class.

4. Dramatize the story of St. Francis and the wolf.

5. Find a picture of St. Francis preaching to the animals.

6. Find a picture of St. Francis receiving the wounds from our Lord on the cross.

7. Imagine that the birds and other animals come to you as they did to St. Francis and write what you would say to them.

8. Tell the class how you can be good to animals.

9. St. Francis loved the sun, the moon, the stars, the trees, and the flowers. Look around today and see how many lovely things you can find. Tell the class what you saw.

10. Read the life of St. Clare and tell the class when her feast is celebrated.

11. Draw a picture for any part of the story of St. Francis.

12. Read the poem "A Thought about St. Francis," by Denis A. McCarthy.

Can you answer these questions?

1. Which is more important, the body or the soul?
2. What is the soul?
3. What gives supernatural life to the soul?
4. How many kinds of grace are there?
5. How is grace lost in the soul?
6. St. Francis and his monks instructed people, admonished sinners, etc. What are these works called?
7. What are the spiritual works of mercy?
8. Why did so many people wish to enter the convent?

Good things to read:

"The Sermon of St. Francis," *De La Salle Reader V,* page 121.

"St. Martin of Tours," *American Cardinal Reader V,* page 247.

"Father Damien," *Rosary Reader V*, page 265.

"A Thought About St. Francis," *Misericordia Reader V,* page 153.

"St. Clare," *A Child's Garden of Religion Stories*, page 243.

"St. Francis and Brother Wolf," *A Child's Garden of Religion Stories*, page 261.

21. The Saint Who Taught the Rosary

What Catholic is there, that does not love the Rosary of Our Lady? It was the great St. Dominic who first taught the rosary. By this beautiful prayer he brought many unbelievers into the Church.

The story is told that one day, when St. Dominic was praying, he complained to our Blessed Lady, that his preaching did so little good. It was at the time of Pope Innocent III, a time when the Church was going through some of her darkest hours. Dominic begged our Lady to save the Church. She appeared to him and gave him the rosary. With beads in hand, he went out once more to preach; and everywhere he went, he taught the people to say the rosary. From that time on his preaching was successful.

Dominic was born in Spain in 1170. Already as a young student he showed his great kindness of heart. One time when a famine broke out and left thousands of people starving, Dominic sold his books, his furniture, and even his clothing, to help them. At another time he offered himself as ransom for a slave.

He became a priest and at the age of twenty-five went to France with his bishop. There they met an abbot from the same convent in which the great St. Bernard had lived more than fifty years before. He was dressed in fine clothing and had many attendants. The abbot complained that in spite of all his preachings, he could not convert the heretics.

"You forget," the two men told him, "that our Lord's disciples went out barefoot to preach to the people, and took nothing with them on their journey."

Dominic's heart was almost broken when he saw how the people of France had lost their faith. He spent the rest of his life in defending the faith and converting sinners.

St. Dominic, Founder of a great Order, receives
the Rosary from our Blessed Lady.

By and by other priests joined him in his work of winning back souls to Christ. When they were not preaching, they lived together like monks in the same house. That was the beginning of the Dominican Order, or the Order of Preachers, as it is sometimes called. The monks wear a white habit and scapular and a black mantle.

Besides the Order of men, St. Dominic also founded an Order for women who wished to live in a convent, and a Third Order for men and women living in the world. The nuns spend their time in teaching the young and the members of the Third Order help the others in defending the rights of the Church by their prayers and good works.

St. Dominic died in the year 1221 and his great Order soon spread all over the world.

Together with St. Francis of Assisi, St. Dominic and his monks helped to make the Church strong and firm at a time when their help was most needed. It was a great work, and it was done by men who, like the disciples of Christ, went out poor and barefoot, and took nothing along on the journey.

Now answer these questions:
1. How did St. Dominic get the rosary?
2. Where was he born?
3. How did he show his love for the poor?
4. How did the Dominican Order have its beginning?
5. What other Orders did St. Dominic found?
6. What is their work?
7. What other great saint lived at the same time?

It was prayer, and especially the rosary, that saved so many souls at the time of St. Dominic. The rosary is still as powerful as it was then.

Can you say the rosary? Sometimes offer the rosary you say for the conversion of sinners. Then you, too, will be joining the great army of men and women who are helping the Church to bring souls to Christ.

Things to do:
1. Find the Feast of St. Dominic on the calendar.
2. St. Catherine of Siena and St. Rose of Lima belonged to the Third Order of St. Dominic. Read their lives and tell the class what you liked best about them. Look for their feasts.
3. Read the life of St. Albert the Great who was a Dominican monk, and find out when he was declared a saint or canonized.
4. Learn the mysteries of the rosary and tell what each mystery is about.
5. Learn a hymn in honor of Mary, Queen of the Rosary.
6. Find the Feast of the Holy Rosary on the calendar.
7. Make a rosary booklet. On the cover put a picture of Mary, Queen of the Rosary, and around it draw a rosary. In the booklet write a few sentences about the fifteen mysteries, each on a separate page, and find a picture to match, if possible.
8. There are many beautiful stories told to show the power of the rosary. If you know one, tell the class about it.

Can you answer these questions?
1. Why was St. Dominic so eager to save souls?
2. Of which should we take greater care, of the body or the soul?
3. Where do the souls of those go who die in mortal sin?
4. What is hell?
5. What should you do if you have committed a mortal sin?

6. What spiritual and corporal works of mercy did St. Dominic perform?

7. In whose honor do we say the rosary?

8. What are the mysteries of the rosary?

9. What is each mystery about?

Good things to read:

"My Beads," *De La Salle Reader V*, page 46.

"St. Dominic," *Misericordia Reader V*, page 5.

"Father McKenna," *Misericordia Reader V*, page 12.

22. Well Hast Thou Written of Me, Thomas

For many days the great St. Thomas had been writing and writing. At last his book was finished. Going to the large crucifix that hung on the wall, he knelt down to pray. Suddenly, a sweet voice spoke to him:

"Well hast thou written of Me, Thomas. What dost thou wish in return?"

It was Jesus Himself speaking to Thomas. The words thrilled the saint's heart. What should he answer?

"I desire no other reward but Thyself, O Lord!" he said. He meant that there was nothing on earth that could satisfy his heart, but God alone. What wonderful things Thomas must have written and what a loving heart he must have had to deserve such words of praise from God Himself. We shall want to hear more about this great man and his work.

Thomas was born of noble parents in Aquino, Italy,

"Well hast thou written of Me, Thomas. What
dost thou wish in return?"

in the year 1226. From early boyhood, he tried his best to keep his heart pure and free from sin. He wished to become a Dominican monk and when he was nineteen years old, received the white habit of the Order. But his family could not bear the thought that this splendid young man should give up wealth and honors and live in a convent. Thomas would not change his mind, however; and so they decided to force him to give up his vocation.

One day when Thomas was on his way to Paris, he was captured and locked up in a castle. What was his surprise to find that his own brothers had brought him back home as their prisoner. Every day his mother and sisters came into his room to try in every possible way to make him give up the thought of being a monk. For two years they kept him a captive; but Thomas would not listen to their promises and threats. When nothing else would help, his brothers tried to make him commit a terrible sin. They did not succeed, however; and God was so pleased with the victory which Thomas had won over evil, that He promised the saint to keep his heart pure all his life.

At last Thomas escaped and went to Cologne to study under the learned St. Albert the Great. From there he went to Paris, where he himself became a famous teacher.

St. Thomas wrote many books about religion. These books are still read and studied by learned men all over the world. We have seen in the beginning of our story, how the Lord Himself was pleased with his writings.

At that time the Church first began to celebrate the Feast of Corpus Christi. Pope Urban IV asked St. Thomas to write the prayers and hymns for this beautiful feast. That is how we come to have the glorious hymns *Lauda Sion,* and *Pange Lingua,* and *Adoro Te* which all good Catholics love to sing before the Blessed Sacrament.

In the year 1274, St. Thomas was called by Pope Gregory to come to the General Council of Lyons. On the way he fell ill. When Holy Viaticum was brought to him, he prayed: "O Jesus, I believe that Thou art present in this sacrament as God and Man. For love of Thee I have labored and lived." Shortly afterward he went to heaven to receive the great reward for which he longed all his life, the Lord God Himself.

Now answer these questions:
1. What did Jesus say to St. Thomas?
2. What did St. Thomas answer?
3. Where was St. Thomas born?
4. What Order did St. Thomas wish to enter?
5. Was his family pleased with his choice?
6. What happened to St. Thomas on his way to Paris?
7. How did his family try to make him change his mind?
8. Who was the great teacher of St. Thomas?
9. What kind of books did St. Thomas write?
10. What hymns did he write?

* * *

The world is so full of lovely things that there should be no room in our lives for evil thoughts or words. We cannot all write great books like St. Thomas Aquinas, but we can speak about God to others and help them to know and love Him. Think of different ways in which you can do this.

St. Thomas loved the Blessed Sacrament and wrote beautiful hymns about it. Learn some of the words which St. Thomas wrote and say or sing them with all your heart when you receive Holy Communion or kneel before the Blessed Sacrament.

Things to do:

1. On the map find Paris and Lyons in France, and Cologne in Germany.

2. Find a picture of St. Thomas Aquinas and let the class see it.

3. Sing the *Tantum Ergo* or *O Salutaris*. The words were written by St. Thomas Aquinas.

4. Look for the Feast of St. Thomas Aquinas on the calendar.

5. Look for the date of the Feast of Corpus Christi for this year. Tell the class what is the meaning of the feast.

6. Look for the lesson about the Council of Nicæa and tell what a General Council is and why it is held.

7. Memorize the words of St. Thomas: "O Jesus, I believe that Thou art present in this sacrament as God and Man," and use them whenever you receive Holy Communion. St. Thomas, the Apostle, also spoke beautiful words which we often use before the Blessed Sacrament. Find the story which tells how Jesus appeared to St. Thomas after His Resurrection and tell what St. Thomas said to Jesus at that time.

Can you answer these questions?

1. St. Thomas is sometimes called the "Angelic Doctor." Why do you think he received that name?

2. What is the Blessed Sacrament?

3. Who instituted the Blessed Sacrament?

4. When was it instituted?

5. What is meant by the Holy Viaticum?

6. Against what commandment do they sin who do not keep their hearts pure?

7. What must you do when you are tempted to commit sin?

8. Can you commit sins with your thoughts?

9. Who knows whether you are committing such sins?

10. May you go with boys or girls who commit sins against the sixth commandment?

11. What should you do to keep your heart pure?

Good things to read:

"The Pope of the Little Children," *Catholic Basic Reader V*, page 202.

"The Legend of the Waxen Ciborium," *De La Salle Reader V*, page 172.

"Sheep and Lambs," *American Cardinal Reader V*, page 210.

"At the Consecration," *American Reader V*, page 11.

"Jesus Rewards His Beloved," *A Child's Garden of Religion Stories*, page 250.

"St. Thomas Aquinas," *American Reader V*, page 29.

O SALUTARIS HOSTIA

St. Thomas Aquinas

O salutaris hostia,
Quae coeli pandis ostium;
Bella premunt hostilia,
Da robur, fer auxilium.

Uni trinoque Domino
Sit sempiterna gloria,
Qui vitam sine termino
Nobis donet in patria. Amen.

TANTUM ERGO

St. Thomas Aquinas

Tantum ergo Sacramentum
Veneremur cernui;
Et antiquum documentum
Novo cedat ritui:
Praestet fides supplementum
Sensuum defectui.

Genitori, Genitoque
Laus et jubilatio,
Salus, honor, virtus quoque
Sit et benedictio:
Procedenti ab utroque
Compar sit laudatio. Amen.

Test Yourself

Twenty-five points make a perfect score.

1. A truth which we cannot fully understand is called a . . . .

2. The . . . . is the third Person of the Blessed Trinity.

3. . . . . is the second Person of the Blessed Trinity.

4. . . . . is the first Person of the Blessed Trinity.

5. . . . . created heaven and earth and all things.

6. Man is composed of . . . . and . . . .

7. Man is made to the image and likeness of . . . .

8. We shall find the chief truths which the Church teaches in the . . . .

9. The .... of man dies, but the .... does not die, because it is a spirit.

10. We must take more care of our .... than of our ....

11. If we lose our .... we lose God and everlasting happiness.

12. God is a .... infinitely perfect.

13. The .... commandment tells us to honor and adore God alone.

14. The sin with which everyone comes into the world is called .... sin.

15. The sacrament which takes away original sin is called ....

16. Original sin is the effect of the sin committed through the disobedience of .... and ....

17. To save Adam and Eve and all of us from the punishment of original sin God promised a ....

18. .... is the promised Redeemer.

19. The Redeemer came to earth on .... day.

20. His mother was ....

21. His foster father was ....

UNIT VII

The Great Revolution

Rulers and princes were often disobedient to the pope, as we have seen, and unfaithful to their promise to protect the Church. Nevertheless, all the people of Europe belonged to one spiritual family, of which the pope was father and head. There was only one religion, and that was the Catholic religion. The children of this great family were sometimes naughty and disobedient, but they knew that they were all branches of the same Vine, and one in the same faith.

But now came a time when the Church was to see her own children separated from her, when many branches were to be torn loose from the true Vine. Martin Luther, a priest and monk, began the terrible rebellion. He refused to take back the false teachings which he had been spreading in Germany and was therefore excommunicated by the pope. Other men soon followed his example. Whole countries separated themselves from the true Church. It was like a great religious Revolution. Men said that the pope had no right to rule them and started religions all their own. They changed some of the Church's teachings so that they could no longer be called Catholics. They received the name "Protestants."

Because the Protestants separated from the true fold, they soon disagreed among themselves and were divided again and again until now there are many different kinds

St. Ignatius.

of Protestants. The Catholic Church, however, is still the same: One, Holy, Catholic, and Apostolic.

Like a good mother, the Church sent out some of her sons, as St. Ignatius, to find the lost sheep and bring them back to the fold. She also did what she could through the Council of Trent, to heal the terrible wounds that she had received from her own children.

23. A Soldier Who Became a Saint

There was war between Spain and France. A Spanish officer lay wounded in a castle. His leg had been shattered and his recovery was very slow. He called for his favorite books, novels about knights and ladies. But there were no such books in this castle, which was the home of a truly Christian knight. They brought him the *Life of Christ* and the *Lives of the Saints*. That was not the kind of reading the proud officer wanted. But what was he to do? He began to turn the pages. He read about St. Francis, the Little Poor Man, about St. Dominic, St. Bernard, and many other heroes of God. How different were their lives from his and how much more worth while for eternity!

"What if some day you were to do what these men did!" he asked himself.

His mind was soon made up.

"I, too, will leave the world and become a saint," he said.

As soon as he was well enough, the officer, whose name was Ignatius Loyola, went to a church and made a confession of all his sins. He gave away his horse and armor, laid his sword on the altar of our Lady, and spent the night in prayer.

Later he went to Jerusalem as a pilgrim. He decided to become a priest, and although he was already thirty-two years old, he studied side by side with the young boys in the Latin school.

Afterwards he went to the University of Paris, where he met a talented Spanish nobleman by the name of Francis Xavier. Whenever Francis spoke about his plans and his future, Ignatius would say to him:

"Francis, 'what doth it profit a man if he gain the whole world, but suffer the loss of his soul!' "

These words so touched the heart of Francis that he decided to leave honors and wealth and join Ignatius in the quest for souls. Four other men had also been won by Ignatius, and together they went to a chapel of our Lady and bound themselves by vows to live a life of poverty and chastity and to go wherever the Holy Father sent them. From now on they called themselves the "Company of Jesus," and joined in the work of the great spiritual army of men who fought bravely to win back the souls which the great Revolution, started by Martin Luther, was tearing away from the Church.

The purpose of the Company of Jesus, or Jesuits, as they are called, is to defend the faith at home and to spread it in other countries. Their motto is, "All for the greater glory of God."

It was not an easy task to work against faithless kings and princes who were separating themselves from the Church with all their people. It was harder than fighting dragons or facing a savage foe. It took years of hard work and still more of suffering, to help the Church Militant keep her children in the true fold. It was sad to see whole countries lost to the faith, for often the poor people did not even know that their leaders were tearing them away from the true Vine. But if at times they could not win back all that fell away from the Church in Europe, they sent great missionaries beyond the seas to other lands to make up for the loss; and we shall see later that the immense harvest of souls in missionary countries was and still is a great joy to the Church.

When St. Ignatius died in 1556, there were already one thousand Jesuits. Their work continues to this day all over the world. Like the many other Orders that were founded before or after them, they are soldiers of Christ and a great blessing to His Church on earth.

Now answer these questions:
1. What kinds of books did Ignatius want to read?
2. Why did they bring him the *Lives of the Saints* and the *Life of Christ?*
3. About whom did he read?
4. What did he decide to do?
5. How old was he when he studied Latin?
6. What did he often say to Francis Xavier?
7. How many men formed the first company?
8. What vows did they take?
9. What did they do for the Church?
10. Why did the Church need their help so much?
11. How many Jesuits were there when St. Ignatius died?

Good reading brought the grace of God to the heart of

Ignatius and made him a great officer in the Company of Jesus. In the time of St. Ignatius there were not many books to be had. It is different now. There is so much good literature in the world today that we shall never be able to read it all, even if we live to be a hundred years old.

It is good to read about all the great heroes and heroines that have done splendid things for the world. It is still better to read about God's saints, who gave their lives to save souls.

Ask yourself:

1. Do I read good books?
2. Do I like to read about God's saints?
3. Do I think about their lives and pray to them sometimes?
4. Do I ever help others to find good reading?
5. Am I careful never to read what is not good?
6. Am I careful never to give others reading that is not good?

Things to do:

1. See whether you have the *Lives of the Saints* at home and read the life of St. Ignatius, July 31.
2. Write a composition about your favorite saint and tell why you like him.
3. Tell the class about a good religious book you have read lately.
4. Bring your favorite magazine to school and tell why you like it.
5. If you do not get a Catholic magazine at home, ask someone to subscribe for one as a Christmas or birthday gift to you. It will seem like a new gift every time it comes.
6. Have an exhibit in your classroom, of all the best Catholic books, magazines, and school papers that you can gather.
7. For your Catholic Reading Exhibit make such posters

as the following: "Read Catholic Books," "The Saints were great heroes. Read their lives."

8. Appoint a committee to give talks about some of the books or magazines you have exhibited.

9. In large letters cut out the following motto for your bulletin board: "All Reading Either Helps or Hurts."

10. Plan with the class what you can do to spread Catholic literature. If there is no Catholic magazine in your own home, begin there.

11. Plan an exchange of Catholic magazines with some of your classmates.

12. Collect good Catholic magazines and bring them to families who do not get any or send them to the missions.

13. Memorize the motto of the Jesuit Fathers: "All for the greater glory of God," and use it to make the good intention during the day. The letters A. M. D. G. stand for the same words in Latin.

Can you answer these questions?

1. What must you do to become a saint?

2. How is the soul of man lost?

3. What causes the supernatural death of the soul?

4. What two sacraments give supernatural life to the soul?

5. What does baptism do for the soul? What does penance do?

6. Can you commit sin by reading? How?

7. How can you tell when a book or magazine is not good reading for you?

8. Suppose you begin reading a book and then find that you get sinful thoughts, what should you do?

9. What do we call the sin by which we lead others to commit sin?

10. How can you lead others into sin?

Good things to read:

"The Soldier Saint," *Cathedral Basic Reader V*, page 184.
"A True Story About a Little Girl," *American Reader V*, page 105.
"Father Marquette," *Catholic Youth Reader VI*, page 142.

24. The Council of Trent

Let us imagine a wide-spreading beautiful vine with lovely green leaves and great winding branches stretching out on all sides. All of a sudden a terrible storm comes up. The wind blows furiously, the lightning flashes, the thunder peals, and large hailstones crash to the ground. When the storm is over, we see a sad picture. Many of the weaker branches have been torn loose and hurled to the ground. Even larger branches have been partly broken away and leaves lie scattered all over the ground.

The storm is the Great Revolution about which we have read. The dried and broken branches are the people who fell away from the Church during the storm. Had they been strong in their faith, they would have held firmly to the vine and the storm could not have hurt them. And now, what is to be done with the sadly damaged vine? A skillful doctor or gardener comes and trims the vine and cuts off the loose and broken branches and cleans away the dead leaves. Then the vine becomes stronger and healthier than before and begins to spread out more gloriously than ever. Such a gardener was the

Council of Trent. With the help of the Holy Ghost this Council did for the Church what the skillful gardener does for the great vine.

When Pope Paul III saw what terrible damage had been done to the Church by the Great Revolution, he called a General Council, which met in the city of Trent. We remember the first General Council which was held in Nicæa. We recall also, that Pope Innocent III called a General Council to meet at the Lateran Palace in Rome. There were other Councils also between, so that this was the nineteenth the Church had held.

There was much to be done; and since there were wars and other troubles, the bishops sometimes had to return home for a time and come back later when the danger was over.

The Church does not teach anything new, we know, when it meets in Council. But, as it often happens, people do not always understand her teachings clearly, and heretics claim their teachings to be true. Then it is the duty of the bishops who meet under the direction of the pope, to explain what the Church expects her children to believe.

During the Great Revolution many false teachings were again spread in Germany and other countries. Now the Council took these teachings one by one, examined them carefully, showed why they were wrong and what is the belief of the Catholic Church. We shall look at a few of the teachings which the Council of Trent explained.

The heretics said there are only two sacraments: Baptism and the Holy Eucharist. The Council of Trent said: "There are seven sacraments although not all are necessary for everybody."

The heretics said: "Christ died for us, and He is our sacrifice. Therefore, we do not need the sacrifice of the Mass." The Catholic Church teaches that in Holy Mass a true sacrifice is offered to God both for the living and the dead.

The heretics said: "There is no purgatory and therefore we need not pray for the dead." The Catholic Church teaches that there is a purgatory and that we can help the Poor Souls by our prayers and good works.

The heretics said: "We do not want the pope as the head of the Church." The Catholics say: "We believe that the pope is the true representative of Jesus Christ on earth and the lawful head of the Church."

During this meeting of the bishops of the whole Catholic world, rules were also made in regard to instructions for the people, the duties of priests and bishops, and the use of the sacramentals. They were intended to help Catholics to lead a better life and become more closely united with the pope, the bishops, and the priests.

And, just as the vine, that seemed badly broken down by the storm, became more healthy and beautiful than ever, so the Church came out of the storm of Revolution with new life and vigor and has continued its wonderful growth down to our own day.

The Council of Trent was called on the thirteenth day

of December, 1545. Once it had to be discontinued for ten years. It was finally ended in December, 1563.

Now answer these questions:
1. To what was the Church compared?
2. What is meant by the storm?
3. Who were the broken branches?
4. Who was the skillful gardener?
5. How many General Councils were held before the Council of Trent?
6. What is the duty of a General Council?
7. Under whose direction must a General Council be?
8. What did the Council teach about the sacraments? About purgatory? About the pope?
9. How did the Church come out of the storm of the Revolution?
10. How long did it take before the Council of Trent was ended?

*   *   *

There are many people today who do not believe as Catholics do. Sometimes they would like to know more about the Catholic Church and what she teaches. Would you be able to answer questions to which every Catholic child should know the answer? Here is a little test for you. If you cannot answer all the questions, be sure to find out the correct answer before you go to the next lesson.
1. How many sacraments are there? Name them.
2. Which sacraments can be received only once?
3. Which sacraments give supernatural life to the soul?
4. Which can be received by men only?
5. Which may be administered by a person not a priest in case of necessity?

6. Which sacraments must be received in the state of grace?

7. Which may be received only in serious illness?

8. Which sacrament is necessary for salvation?

9. What is the sacrifice of the Mass?

10. Why do Catholics have to go to Mass on Sundays and Holydays?

11. Who said the first Mass?

12. Who are the Poor Souls?

13. What can we do to help the Poor Souls?

14. Can the Poor Souls commit sin?

15. Can the Poor Souls still be lost?

16. Who made the pope the head of the Church?

17. What is the name of the present pope?

18. Where does he live?

19. Can the pope commit sin?

20. Does the pope have to go to confession?

21. To whom does he go?

22. Does the pope tell Catholics for whom they should vote?

UNIT VIII

The Church, Mother of Art and Learning

The Church that brought the faith to the barbarian nations, also brought them civilization and learning. We know that the monks taught the trades and the arts; and, as they taught, they reminded the people that their gifts of body and mind were given to them for the honor and glory of God. It is no wonder, then, that, as the nations became Christian, they honored God not only with their lips but also with their works. It is no wonder that the trades and arts developed into something finer and nobler every year.

Especially in the second half of the Middle Ages we find much to marvel at in art and learning. There were great schools and universities, where law, medicine, literature, and many other subjects were taught. There were brilliant teachers like St. Thomas Aquinas, whose books are studied to this day. There were wonderful cathedrals where the people daily met and worshiped God. Sculptors carved statues of perfect beauty; artists painted pictures that have never been equaled; and Dante, the poet, wrote the *Divine Comedy* which is called the greatest religious poem that was ever written.

In the following lessons we shall hear more about some of the great works inspired by the Church during the Middle Ages.

25. The Church and Schools

Young children did not always go to school as they do today. There was a time many, many years ago, when most boys and girls were taught the useful things of life at home by their mothers. Life was simple; there was little use for reading or writing and no use for geography and history and the many other lessons you learn today. The boys learned to hunt, and to ride, and to fight. The girls learned to spin, to sew, and to take care of the household. The only ones that needed higher learning were those who were to become priests.

You remember reading about the barbarians that overran Europe and destroyed everything as they went along. The Church, like a good mother, took these barbarian children and taught them how to live as good Christians. Whatever there remained of learning in those days was found in the Church. Everything else had gone to ruin. If it had not been for the monks in the monasteries, many of the most valuable books would have been lost forever.

If, then, we are to find schools, we shall have to look in the monasteries, where boys were being prepared for the priesthood. And what an interesting place the monastery schools were. There were monks copying old, old books by hand, letter by letter. Some pages were made

A section of an early manuscript Bible.

very beautiful by large capital letters done in gold and bright-colored inks, with designs all along the sides. There were other monks making models of churches, and towers, and bridges, and still others carving statues or painting pictures. There were those who wrote the history of the past, or studied how to preach the gospel, or to make medicine, or to raise better crops.

By and by the cathedral schools were founded, where boys learned singing and religion, also reading, writing, grammar, and other subjects. These schools were open to all boys whether they intended to become priests or not. They often had famous masters. We remember the great men that Charlemagne called to teach in his palace school, which was much like the cathedral schools. When the nobles heard of some great school in a distant city, they often sent their sons there so that they might have the best teachers.

As we come to the twelfth and thirteenth centuries, we find in some of the largest cities great schools having thousands of students from all parts of Europe. These schools were called universities and, like the earlier schools, were under the direction of the Church.

It was in the Middle Ages that some of the most wonderful teachers the world has ever had were to be found in the universities. The University of Paris was, in time, considered the greatest of all, and no one, no matter to what country he belonged, could say that his education was complete, unless he had studied in Paris at least for some years. Other important universities were at Salerno and Bologna in Italy, and Oxford and Cambridge in England. St. Albertus Magnus was one of the great teachers, and St. Thomas Aquinas, his pupil, was even more famous.

It was the Church that gave us learning from the earliest schools to the great universities of the Middle Ages, and that is the reason why she is called the Mother of Learning.

Now answer these questions:

1. Where were children taught the useful things of life in the early ages?

2. For whom were the monastery schools?

3. What did the monks do in the monastery schools?

4. Which schools were founded next?

5. What were the great schools of the Middle Ages called?

6. Where were some of the great universities of the Middle Ages?

7. Who were two of the great teachers?

*   *   *

Things to do:

1. Imagine that you lived in the days before children learned to read or write. Tell the class how you spent the day.

2. Write about a visit to an old monastery school and tell what you saw there.

3. Read the lesson about Charlemagne once more and find what it says about the palace school. Who were some of the great teachers of that school?

4. On the map locate the cities where the great universities were.

5. In a history of the early times read about the Migration of Nations. Tell the class what you have read.

6. Find out something about the history of your school. Here are a few points to talk or write about:

a) Our school.

b) The first pastor of our school.
c) The first teachers of our school.
d) The patron of our school.
e) Why we are proud of our school.
f) Our teachers.
g) Our priests.
7. Choose one of your classmates to give a talk on the following: "Why I should go to a Catholic school."

Can you answer these questions?
  1. How do children learn to know their religion?
  2. Why must they learn their religion?
  3. What commandment tells you to obey your parents?
  4. Whom else must you obey?
  5. What would you expect of a good pupil of your school?

26. St. John Baptist de la Salle

Madam de la Salle wondered where her little boy John Baptist was. With so many noble guests in the house and all the music and dancing, she had quite forgotten about him. She must send a servant to find him.

In a quiet room away from all the noise and laughter, the little boy sat with eager, upturned face, listening to the stories his grandmother was reading to him. He had slipped over to her during the feasting and dancing and had asked her to come away and read to him.

And what were the stories that John Baptist listened to with so much pleasure? They were the *Lives of the Saints*. To him their noble deeds of self-denial and penance and their adventures in the search for souls, were more thrilling than those of proud knights who fought for nothing but a little honor. Perhaps it was already then that the little boy made up his mind that he, too,

St. John Baptist de la Salle.

would be a saint. At any rate, he loved to talk to God in prayer and tried to keep his soul free from sin.

Playing priest was one of his favorite occupations and it was a happy day when he was allowed for the first time to be a real server at the altar. But in spite of all that we have heard, John Baptist was every inch a boy. He played and studied and enjoyed himself just as boys do today. If there was anything in his life that made him very dear to God, it was that he did all the little duties of every day as well as he knew how; and every boy and girl can do that easily enough.

On the day of his First Holy Communion John Baptist heard the call of God to become a priest. From that time on he prepared himself with his whole heart for this wonderful vocation. He kept two things always in mind: he must become a learned man, and he must become a holy man. And for that reason he studied in the best schools of France and at the same time practiced every virtue necessary for a man who desires to receive Holy Orders.

Holy Saturday came, the happiest day in the long and troubled life of John Baptist de la Salle. It was on that day in 1678, in the city of Rheims, that he walked up to the altar of God as a priest and spoke for the first time those solemn words that call Christ down from heaven to be the food of men.

John Baptist hoped from that day on to spend his life in preaching, hearing confessions, and in the duties of the priesthood. If someone had asked him whether he ever thought of spending the rest of his life in a schoolroom and in training teachers, he would most probably have laughed at the thought. And yet, that is exactly what God wanted of him.

In those days there were very few schools for the poor. The colleges and universities were intended for the children of the nobility. A few good priests took the time to teach the children of the common people, but they had many other duties, and could not do much. The little girls of Rheims were being taken care of by some pious women who later became known as the Sisters of the Holy Child Jesus. The boys were almost entirely neglected.

One day a man by the name of Nyel came to Rheims to start a school for boys. He went to John Baptist de la Salle for help and advice. The saint knew that if good schools were to be opened, there would also have to be good teachers. But there were none to be had. The men who were teaching in the few common schools up to this time, knew little more than their pupils. Therefore it became necessary to train teachers for the work. No one was better fitted for this task than John Baptist de la Salle.

We shall never know the many sacrifices John Baptist de la Salle had to make to carry on this work. He brought the new teachers into his own beautiful home and taught them not only their lessons but also their manners. For in those days the common people, to whom these teachers belonged, had no training. They were good at heart but often rude and thoughtless. Later John Baptist even gave away his great wealth to the poor so that he might become more like the men whom he was trying to teach.

From the time that de la Salle began to train teachers, schools grew everywhere. But God's work often brings sorrow and disappointment with it. Hardly were these men ready to teach, when they began to feel that they were able to earn more money if they worked for themselves. And had the saint thought only of himself, he would have dropped the work right there. He was thinking of the honor of God, however, and the souls of the poor boys.

Then he began to see that if his schools were to have the right kind of teachers, they would have to bind themselves by some kind of promise to stay together. That is why de la Salle brought together the twelve leading teachers of his schools on the Feast of the Ascension in 1684. He wanted to pray with them and plan with them so that they might know the best way of continuing the work of Christian education. On Trinity Sunday the first twelve Brothers of the Christian Schools, as they called themselves, knelt before the altar in their little chapel and promised God by vow to remain together for one year. There were to be no priests among them, for their lives were to be spent entirely in prayer, teaching, and study. At the end of the year they could again make their vows.

When de la Salle founded the Brothers of the Christian Schools, he did something that had never been done before. There had never been a society of men who gave their entire lives to the teaching of boys, without becoming priests or doing other work besides. It was a work that was much needed at the time, and because it was entirely according to the will of God, it spread rapidly into different cities and countries. In our own country thousands of boys attend the splendid schools of the Christian Brothers and many in turn follow the example of their teachers and give up all they have to lead a life of prayer, teaching, and study.

After a life of hard work, of few joys, and many disappointments, de la Salle died on Good Friday, April 7, 1719. He was 68 years old. Pope Leo XIII placed his name among those of the saints in 1900. His feast is celebrated on May 15.

Now answer these questions:

1. What kind of stories did John Baptist de la Salle like best?
2. What did he like to play?
3. When did he first hear the call of God?
4. What two things did he always keep in mind?
5. On what day did he say his first Holy Mass?
6. To what work did God call him?
7. By whom were the little girls being taught in Rheims?
8. Who was best fitted to train teachers for the boys' schools?
9. What did he have to teach these men besides their lessons?
10. With how many men did the saint found the Brothers of the Christian Schools?
11. For how long did they at first promise to remain together?
12. Why was his society different from others?

13. When did John Baptist de la Salle die?
14. When is his feast?

*   *   *

John Baptist de la Salle felt that he was responsible to God for all he had received. Therefore he made the best possible use of his wealth, his time, and his talents. You, too, are responsible to God for all He has given to you. Do you realize that God's gifts to you are precious and may not be wasted?

Show how the following children are responsible for gifts which God has given them.

1. Charlie Lamb is very bright. When he listens to the children reciting in school, he learns enough to get by without studying. He just manages to pass his grade each year.

2. Eddie Bell catches cold easily. He has been ill very much. His mother tells him he must always wear a slicker when it rains, but he will not do it.

3. Nellie Kemp takes piano lessons. Her mother has to work extra for the money it costs. Whenever Nellie gets a chance, she skips practice. She says it does not make any difference to her whether she ever learns any music.

4. The children of St. Patrick's School get two hours for study every day. Tom and Dick spend most of this time playing and teasing the other pupils.

5. Anna Mann and her twin brother are in the same grade. Anna finds it easy to study, but her brother does not. Do you think Anna should do her brother's homework for him? What can she do?

6. Mert Brady can sing well. Grandmother likes to hear him sing, but he always says he has no time.

7. Della Mohr's mother is called out of town for a few days and Della has to take care of the house. There is no

one there but grandfather. What are some of the things Della might do?

8. Father Lord wants to start an orchestra. Billy Trainor can play the trumpet and is asked to join. Billy refuses because he does not like to give up his playtime for practice.

9. Jamie Wells has just received a beautiful new book for his birthday. He leaves it out on the lawn and does not feel like going out in the evening to get it.

10. Pauline Barton asks her mother for a plot of garden all her own. She buys seed to raise some vegetables. She does not water the plants, however, and they dry out.

Things to do:

1. Read about the city of Rheims in France and find what it is noted for.

2. John Baptist de la Salle did all his little duties well. Make a list of the duties you have each day.

3. Recite the words which are spoken by the priest at consecration and tell what happens at that moment.

4. Find the names of other saints mentioned in this book, who gave away their wealth and became poor for God.

5. What do we call the beautiful trait of character which makes some people give their money and time for others? Tell of some ways in which you can show the same trait.

6. Write a list of other saints who founded Orders and give the name of the Order in each case.

7. Boys and girls of today should learn good manners early. Tell how you can practice good manners in school, at home, in company, on the street, in the street car. Is there any one of them that you have forgotten to practice. Do you say "Please" and "Thank you"? Start again today.

Can you answer these questions?

1. What vocation did John Baptist follow?
2. What sacrament did he receive when he became a priest?
3. What kind of mark does this sacrament leave on the soul?
4. What is the holiest act a priest performs each day?
5. What is the Mass?
6. What is a sacrifice?
7. In what way is the sacrifice of the Mass the same as the sacrifice on the cross?
8. What difference is there between the two?
9. How should we hear Mass?
10. When must we hear Mass?
11. What are the holydays of obligation?
12. What commandment tells us to keep the Sabbath holy?
13. What may we not do on Sundays?

Good things to read:

"A Hymn of Praise," *Cathedral Basic Reader V*, page 99.
"A Hymn to St. La Salle," *De La Salle Reader V*, page 3.
"The Use of Flowers," *De La Salle Reader V*, page 30.
"Blow, Blow, Thou Winter Wind," *Catholic Education Series V*, page 89.

27. Michelangelo

A happy day dawned for the boy Michelangelo. He was told by his master under whom he was studying art in the city of Florence, that he and his friend were in-

Michelangelo's statue of Moses.

vited to the garden of a prince. As he walked through that wonderful garden and saw the old Greek statues so beautifully carved from marble, a whole world of art seemed to open before him; for ever since his early childhood, he had loved to work and play with marble. There were blocks of marble standing ready, and Michelangelo and his friend were told they might use them to copy anything they chose. There was nothing that could have made them happier.

One day the great Prince Lorenzo was walking through the garden. He saw Michelangelo sculpturing the head of an old faun.

"You have made your faun old," he said, "and yet you have left all the teeth. At such an age some of the teeth are usually out."

The boy said nothing. The next time the prince passed by, he saw that some of the teeth had been carefully broken out of the faun's head. He was so pleased because Michelangelo had taken his advice, that he asked the lad to come and live with him in the palace.

And so we find the young sculptor dressed in fine clothes and daily sitting at table with princes. Here he worked for several years, when to his great sorrow, Prince Lorenzo died.

From that time on Michelangelo worked both in Rome and in Florence. When he was only 24 years old, he carved a statue which is one of the finest he ever made in his life. It is called the "Pieta" and represents the dead Christ lying in the arms of the Mother of Sorrows.

Two other figures of Michelangelo's that have become well known to all who love art, are the statues of David and of Moses. The statue of David was made for the city of Florence. Picture to yourself an immense rough block of marble standing in the artist's workshop. A wooden tower is built around it, and the sculptor shuts himself up in it so that nobody may see him work. Right and left fly the chips, as the artist works with all his might. In his soul he can already see the vision of the young David standing before him, and he can hardly wait to see the form come out of the marble block. At last the wooden tower is removed, and all Florence is filled with joy and wonder. Before them, in pure white marble, stands the beautiful David just ready to kill the giant Goliath.

Even more famous is the statue of Moses, which was ordered by Pope Julius II. It is an immense figure showing Moses just after he has come down from the mountain. He must be looking at the Israelites worshiping the golden calf, for his face has a fiery expression, and he seems to be holding himself back from springing forward in anger at sight of the idolatry of his people.

Michelangelo had always felt that he was a sculptor and nothing else. But now the pope sent for him to paint the ceiling of the Sistine chapel in the Vatican.

"I am not a painter, but a sculptor," Michelangelo said.

"A man such as you is everything that he wishes to be," replied the pope.

"But this is work for Raphael, the painter," said Michelangelo. "Give him this room to paint and give me a mountain to carve."

But the pope was firm, and Michelangelo had to put aside his chisel and take up the brush.

The ceiling of the chapel was high and arched, and Michelangelo had to do much of the painting lying flat on his back.

Michelangelo loved to read his Bible, and it was the stories of the Bible that he painted on the ceiling. In all there are over three hundred figures, most of them more than life size. Although, as we know, Michelangelo claimed sculpture to be his real work, many artists say that these paintings are his finest works.

How much the work of this great artist was admired and how eager people were to have him express his wonderful ideas in marble, can be seen from the following: When Paul III became pope he said: "I have desired for ten years to be pope that I might make Michelangelo work for me alone, and now I will not be disappointed." Yet in spite of his fame, Michelangelo was a stern, quiet man, who lived most of his life alone.

We have seen Michelangelo as a sculptor and painter; he was also a poet and architect. He wrote beautiful poems and in his old age was made architect for the great St. Peter's Church in Rome. He refused to accept any pay from the pope for this work, however, saying that he was doing it for the glory of God.

Michelangelo died in Rome in 1564 at the age of 89.

His body was carried to his beloved city of Florence, where he was buried in the Church of the Holy Cross. He had played a noble part in making the sixteenth century the "Golden Age" of Italian art. If you ever visit Italy you will want to see some of his wonderful statues and especially his famous paintings on the ceiling of the Sistine chapel in the Vatican. You will recall, then, that it was mostly through the popes that these great masterpieces were made. The Church is truly the Mother of Art.

Now answer these questions:

1. In whose garden was Michelangelo invited to work?
2. Why was the prince pleased with him?
3. How old was Michelangelo when he carved the Pieta?
4. What other statues did he carve?
5. Who asked him to paint the ceiling of the chapel?
6. Why did Michelangelo not want to do the work?
7. What kind of pictures did he paint?
8. Why would he not take any pay as architect of St. Peter's?

*   *   *

Michelangelo was one of the world's greatest artists. It is said that a friend once asked him what he had done on one of his statues since the last time he saw it. Michelangelo told him he had done a great deal. He had made a little change here, and put a touch there, and so on.

"Yes," said the friend, "but those are all trifles."

"Trifles make perfection, but perfection is no trifle," answered the artist.

Can you tell what the words mean?

"Whatever is worth doing at all is worth doing well," says a proverb. Do you do all your daily tasks well?

Ask yourself:

Do I pray well?

Do I do the very best I can in my schoolwork?

Do I study my lessons until I am sure I know them well?

Do I do my work at home with pleasure and as well as I can?

Do I write my tasks as neatly and carefully as I can?

Look over any work you did today and see whether it was done as perfectly as you can do it. If not, perhaps you can still change it.

Things to do:

1. Find Florence on the map.

2. See how many pictures you can find of Michelangelo's statues and paintings.

3. Find out whether there is a Pieta or Sorrowful Mother statue in your church. Do you think it would be easy to cut such a statue out of a block of stone?

4. In the Old Testament find the story of David fighting Goliath and of the Israelites adoring the golden calf. Tell the stories in class.

5. Which Bible stories do you think Michelangelo might have painted on the ceiling of the chapel? Write the titles of as many stories as you can remember.

6. Do you like to carve? Some people carve lovely little articles out of Ivory soap. Perhaps you would like to try it. If you have never tried it, start with something simple like a cross, or a star.

Can you answer these questions?

1. Why do we sometimes call Mary the Sorrowful Mother?

2. What are some of the sorrows Mary suffered?

3. Which are the sorrowful mysteries of the rosary?
4. Why did Christ die for us?
5. How long did He remain in the grave?
6. Where was His soul during that time?
7. What is Limbo?
8. On what day did Christ rise from the dead?
9. Do people ever adore idols now?
10. What is superstition?
11. What superstitious beliefs do you know?

Good things to read:
"The Sculptor," *Ideal Reader V*, page 101.
"The Snow Madonna," *Rosary Reader IV*, page 255.

28. Raphael

About five centuries ago, so the legend tells us, there lived a venerable old hermit among the Italian hills near Rome. People called him Father Bernardo. One day a terrible storm arose, so terrible, in fact, that Father Bernardo would have been killed had it not been for the shelter of an old oak tree into whose branches he crept, and for the help of Mary, the beautiful daughter of a wine dresser, who sent her father to save him. The old hermit prayed that some day God would reward both the tree and the girl.

Years passed by. The hermit died and the oak tree was made into wine casks for Mary's father. One day Mary, now the mother of two lovely children, was sitting in the garden near one of these casks, with her baby held close in her arms. An older child came running toward her with a cross made out of two sticks. Just then Raphael, the great artist passed by. He was thinking of a picture of our Lady which he had to paint, and wondering where he could find a model. He noticed the beautiful mother with her two children. Here was the model he was looking for. Picking up the cover of the wine cask, he drew a picture of the mother and children on it and then took it home to paint in colors.

You have often seen a copy of this lovely picture. It is called the *Madonna della Sedia* or the *Madonna of the Chair*. The painting now hangs in the art gallery of Florence, Italy, where you will see it, should you ever travel that way.

But there is another painting by Raphael which is even greater than this one. It is said to be the most beautiful Madonna picture that was ever painted. You have seen copies of it many times. It is called the *Sistine Madonna*.

The painting of the *Sistine Madonna* hangs in the art gallery at Dresden in a room all by itself. When people walk into that room and look at the beautiful Mother with the Child in her arms, they always become silent. It seems to them as if the two figures in the picture were alive and ready to move.

Perhaps you have never noticed how wonderful these two pictures really are. That may be because what you have seen are only copies, which can never show the

Raphael's Sistine Madonna.

true beauty of the paintings made by Raphael himself. Some day you will have to see these and many other paintings for yourself and marvel at the sweet faces and lovely colors.

Raphael, the great artist whose pictures have become the wonder of the world, was born in the city of Urbino in Italy on Good Friday of the year 1483. His father gave him his first lessons in painting at home and soon found that the little boy had wonderful talent. Therefore he sent him to study under Perugino, one of the great masters living in Italy at that time. It was not long before the pupil became more skilled than the master.

Like all Italian artists of that time, Raphael longed to go to Florence, the great center of art. There he saw the works of such masters as Leonardo and Michelangelo and learned from them to improve his own paintings. In Florence he began to paint the many Madonna pictures which the whole world knows and loves.

But it was in Rome that Raphael was to find his greatest glory. Pope Julius II was just having the Vatican repainted, and he called for the young artist to come and do his share. Here Raphael painted beautiful pictures on the walls and on the ceiling of the Vatican gallery. The pictures on the ceiling were scenes from the Bible and are often spoken of as "Raphael's Bible."

Raphael was a handsome man with a kind heart and a charming manner. Everybody loved him. Wherever he went, his pupils and friends were around him listening to his words and watching him at his work. Every morning when he walked from his home to the Vatican, fifty painters were with him. At the same time another artist could be seen going to his work all by himself. It was the silent, lonely Michelangelo, who had also been called by the pope, to help with the decoration of the Vatican.

The great cardinals of Rome all wanted Raphael to paint for them, for he had become the greatest of all masters. He worked in Rome for twelve years and was kept so busy teaching and painting that his body was soon worn out. He lived to be only 37 years old, but in his short life he painted 287 pictures. Most of these are pictures of the Madonna and Child, for there is no subject he loved to paint more than that.

On Good Friday, April 6, at nine o'clock in the evening, he went to his eternal rest. All the people of the city deeply mourned his loss, and the pope himself wept bitterly.

Now answer these questions:

1. What legend is told about Father Bernardo?
2. Who was the artist that drew a picture of Mary and her children?
3. What is the name of this picture?
4. What other Madonna picture is well known?
5. Where is the picture of the *Sistine Madonna* now?
6. On what day was Raphael born and on what day did he die?
7. In what city did Raphael begin his great Madonna pictures?

8. Who called Raphael to Rome? Why?

9. How long did he work in Rome?

10. How many pictures did he paint in his short life?

11. What kind of pictures did he most like to paint?

*   *   *

How much Raphael must have loved the Mother of God and her divine Son, to be able to paint such wonderful pictures of them, and how pleased Mary must have been with him and his work.

What can you do to show your love for Mary, the Mother of God? How can you paint the picture of Christ and Mary on your soul? Say the Hail Mary with great devotion today.

Give a little program in honor of Mary, the Mother of God. Use any hymns, poems, and prayers to Mary that you know. Here are a few hints. You may change whatever you like.

A Hymn to Mary.

Poems in honor of Mary:

"The Annunciation" — Adelaide A. Procter.

"The Child of Mary's Prayer" — Rev. F. C. Kolbe.

"A Visit to the Dresden Art Gallery" (composition by one of the pupils).

The Legend of the Monk Bernardo.

Hymn to Mary.

My Favorite Picture of Mary (composition by one of the class).

Poems:

"When Mary Went Walking" — Denis McCarthy.

"The Mother's Quest" — Rev. Hugh F. Blunt.

Hail Mary, sung or prayed.

In the classroom put up as many different pictures of the Madonna as you can find.

Make a Madonna book for yourself. In it paste as many

172 THE VINE AND THE BRANCHES

different Madonna pictures as you can find. Do not be in a hurry to finish the book but keep the collection and add pictures from year to year. Try to learn the names and artists of the best-known pictures.

Or, if you would rather, make a poem book in honor of Mary by collecting poems written about her.

Can you answer these questions?
1. Who is the Blessed Virgin Mary?
2. How did Jesus Christ become man?
3. On what day was He born?
4. Why did He become man?
5. Was Jesus Christ always God?
6. How do you know that He is true God?
7. How many natures are there in Jesus Christ?
8. How many persons are there in Jesus Christ?

Good things to read:
"The Lord Is with Thee," *Cathedral Basic Reader V,* page 201.
"Peter of Cortona," *De La Salle Reader V,* page 110.
"The O of Giotta," *Misericordia Reader V,* page 221.
"The Cardinal's Lodger," *Misericordia Reader V,* page 226.

29. The Cathedral Builders

The Church has always taught her children to give their best to God. Whatever work they did, therefore, for the service of God, was done with much joy and without the thought of pay. Nor were the builders and artists satisfied with what they had done once; they always tried to produce better and finer work. They did not think of having their names known or of receiving praise and honor. Their minds and hearts were lifted up to God for whom alone they worked. No wonder they produced works of art and particularly churches, at sight of which people of today can only stand in admiration.

The art of church building reached its highest perfection between the eleventh and fifteenth centuries. Wherever there was a town of some importance, a cathedral had to be built to crown its glory. Many of the people in the town helped together at these buildings. Priests worked with masons, painters, and sculptors, and all of them put into every inch of space the best that was in them. But these great churches were not built in a few years. There was very little machinery so that everything had to be done by hand. It took several hundred years to finish the work, but it was done for the ages. If we were to visit Europe today, we would be shown with pride, the great Gothic cathedrals, built centuries ago, and still the wonder of the world.

These wonderful cathedrals were not intended for great monuments only. A church was to be a worthy home for God. Every day at Mass, Christ, the Redeemer, came down from heaven to offer Himself again for mankind. The whole world, therefore, was to be represented around the altar of sacrifice. Plants and animals, men

One of the great Gothic cathedrals of the Middle Ages,
a picture of beauty and faith.

and angels, all were the work of the Creator and were to pay Him honor through symbols or pictures. Symbols were used a great deal more in the Middle Ages than today, and every child knew their meaning. Every church was like a stone book from which all might read. In fact, when these Gothic cathedrals were built there were no printed books and only a few people could read.

Every bit of work, therefore, from the lofty spires to the smallest ornaments, was meant to be of some service. It was intended to lift the heart to God and to teach the great truths of religion. When people approached a town, long before the houses could ever be seen, the spires seemed to cry out to the travelers: "Lift up your hearts." The building itself was in the shape of a cross, reminding them of the sign of their redemption. On the outside of the cathedral high up on the walls and among the towers and eaves, hideous creatures were carved. They are called gargoyles and represent the evil spirits flying away at the coming of Christ.

The simple-hearted people also learned many of the truths of religion from the stained-glass windows, the statues in the niches, and the paintings on the ceilings and walls. Indeed, every little ornament or design was so full of meaning, that someone has said that it would take more than a lifetime to study everything that a single one of these cathedrals had to teach us.

The Gothic cathedrals of the Middle Ages are pictures of perfect beauty. Those best known are the cathedrals of Rheims, Paris, Chartres, Amiens, Lincoln, Exeter, Westminster, Cologne, and Freiburg.

Love of God and gratitude for His favors inspired the world's greatest cathedrals. They are the Church's gift to the world. How glorious is the Church in all her works.

Now answer these questions:

1. With what intention has the Church taught her children always to work?

2. When did the art of church building reach its highest perfection?

3. How long did it take to build some of the great cathedrals?

4. Why were they built so carefully and beautifully?

5. What does the spire mean?

6. In what shape is the building?

7. How did the people, who could not read, learn their religion?

8. In what cities are some of these great cathedrals?

9. What inspired the great cathedrals of the world?

*   *   *

The church steeple reminds us to lift up our hearts. It tells us to think of God and pray to Him. Everything in a church should help us to keep our minds on God and holy things. Prayer is necessary for everybody. We should pray every morning and evening; before and after meals; on Sundays and holydays; in times of necessity, sickness, and temptation.

Ask yourself:

Do I pray often?

Do I think of what I am saying when I pray?

Do I pray for my parents?

Do I pray for the Church, the pope, and the priests?

Do I pray for sinners?

Do I pray for the souls in purgatory?

Do I pray for my brothers and sisters, for my friends, for my teachers?

Do I sometimes talk to God and the saints all by myself and in my own words?

Do I say my morning and night prayers?

Do I pray before and after meals?

Do I pray at once when I am tempted?

Watch yourself today at your prayers and try to say them as well as you can. Tonight when you examine your conscience, ask yourself whether you prayed with devotion.

Things to do:

1. If you have stained-glass windows in your church, have different pupils select a window and tell the story it teaches.

2. You will find many symbols in church, on the altar, on the walls, and in the windows. Of how many do you know the meaning?

3. Read about one of the great cathedrals of the world and tell the class what you have read.

4. Find pictures of some of the great cathedrals and talk about them in class.

5. If there are any paintings in your church tell the class about one of them.

6. Imagine you are visiting in one of the great cathedrals of Europe. Write a letter to your class telling what you have seen.

7. Look up the word *gargoyle* in the dictionary. Perhaps you can find a picture of a gargoyle to show to the class.

8. Look in the Mass prayers and find when the words "Lift up your hearts" are said.

9. Pay a visit to some neighboring church that has interesting statues, windows, or paintings and tell the class what you have seen.

10. Memorize the following: "Watch ye, and pray that ye enter not into temptation" (Matt. xxvi. 41). "Amen, Amen I say to you: if you ask the Father anything in My name, He will give it to you" (John xvi. 23).

Can you answer these questions?

1. Why did the people make their churches so beautiful?
2. What great sacrifice is offered each day in the Catholic Church?
3. What is prayer?
4. How should we pray?
5. When should we pray?
6. Do we always receive what we pray for?
7. Which are the principal prayers a Catholic should know?
8. Which prayer did our Lord Himself teach?
9. What is a symbol?
10. Name some symbols and give their meaning.

Good things to read:

"The Gothic Cathedral," *Shield's Religion Book IV,* page 85.

"What the Gothic Cathedral Taught the People," *Shield's Religion Book IV,* page 109.

"The Church of Gold," *Rosary Reader V,* page 290.

"For the Honor of the City," *American Cardinal Reader V,* page 114.

"Prayer," *Shield's Reader V,* page 235.

Test Yourself

Twenty points is a perfect score.

1. What Christian emperor had great teachers from other countries in his Palace School? . . . .

2. The Holy Land was in the hands of the Turks whose religion was called after their prophet . . . .

3. The holy wars against the Turks were called . . . .

4. Every one who went to the holy wars wore a . . . . on his shoulder.

5. The Holy Land is also called . . . .

6. The cry of the first crusaders was . . . .

7. The king who did penance before Pope Gregory VII at Canossa was . . . .

8. Pope Innocent III built a . . . . called *Santo Spiritu.*

9. St. Bernard was called by the pope to preach a . . . .

10. The Little Poor Man of Assisi founded the . . . . Order.

11. Many people were converted by St. Dominic through the . . . . which the Blessed Mother taught him.

12. St. Thomas Aquinas wrote beautiful hymns in honor of the . . . .

13. The order which St. Ignatius Loyola founded was called the Company of . . . .

14. The people who tore themselves away from the Church during the Great Revolution are called . . . .

15. The Church became stronger and healthier again after the Council of . . . .

16. The arts and trades were taught in monasteries by the . . . .

17. The statue of David was made by . . . .

18. Art in the Middle Ages developed chiefly through the encouragement of great . . . .

19. The paintings called "Raphael's Bible" can be seen in the . . . .

20. The great . . . . cathedrals were built for the glory of God.

UNIT IX

The Church and the Nations

When Jesus founded the Church, He told the Apostles to go and teach all nations. We know that the Apostles, in obedience to this command, went to distant countries to teach the people the Christian faith. When they died, others took their places and carried the teachings of Christ to still farther countries. From those early times to this very day missionaries have been busy teaching and converting the nations, many of them giving their lives for their faith.

Sometimes, after many years of labor, the missionaries would have to start all over again. That is what happened after the migration of nations. At other times, as when Luther began to spread his false teachings, the Church would send out her best men to defend the faith or to win back the lost sheep of the fold of Christ. Always the Church works and prays for those peoples and nations that have not yet learned to know the teachings of Christ. She longs to be the mother of all so that all might learn to know God, to love and serve Him here on earth, and to be happy with Him in heaven.

We shall now go back and follow the work of some of the great missionaries, from the early days of St. Patrick down to the years of discovery in America.

30. St. Patrick

On a green hillside of a fertile and beautiful island sat a 16-year-old boy, watching his herd. His thoughts were far, far away to the north with his father and mother. Were they still living, he wondered? Did they think sometimes of their son Patrick and wonder whether they would ever see him again? It was six years now since he had been captured and brought to Ireland as a slave. And yet, how good God had been to him during that time! Here in the great open spaces, alone with his herd, he had felt himself drawn closer to God. He had learned to pray not only with his lips but also with his heart.

Yonder, not so many miles away, was the Western Sea. If only he could get away unseen, perhaps he could board a vessel and find his way back home. Why not? A great longing arose in Patrick's heart, and it grew from day to day until he could no longer resist. And so one night he crept away and ran as fast as he could, toward the sea. A trading vessel was ready to set sail. Patrick begged the men to take him along, but they refused, perhaps because he was too poor to pay. Sadly he turned away. What was he to do?

All at once he heard someone calling him. The men on the vessel were telling him to come back. With a happy heart he boarded the ship. He was going home!

After leaving the vessel, Patrick had to wander around a long time before he found his home again. But he reached there at last and was happy to be with his parents and friends once more.

But the beautiful green Isle, where he had so long been a captive, could not be forgotten. In his dreams he could hear the good Irish folk calling to him to come back and walk among them once more. At last he felt that God wished him to be a missionary to Ireland, where most of the people were still pagans. For more than fifteen years he prayed and studied in order to prepare himself for this great work. He became a parish priest and later a bishop.

Patrick was then ready to go back to the beautiful island he had learned to love. He set sail with a few companions and at once began his work of preaching the Gospel. He knew the language and the customs of the people and therefore gained their confidence wherever he went. His first care was to preach to the chiefs or kings, because he knew that if they were converted, their people would soon follow.

The story is told that at one time when Patrick was preaching, the king would not accept the mystery of the Blessed Trinity. Then Patrick bent down and picked up a tiny shamrock. "Just as on the shamrock there are three leaves and only one stem," he said, "so are the three divine Persons only one God." Ever since that time the shamrock is especially dear to the Irish people; and every year on St. Patrick's Day, they wear one in his honor.

St. Patrick traveled all over Ireland, and wherever he went, he baptized the people, built churches, and ordained priests. He also founded great monasteries where men and women spent their lives in serving God, in studying holy books, and in teaching others the way to heaven. No wonder, then, that the former pagan island came, in time, to be known as the Island of Saints.

What made St. Patrick so successful in his work as a missionary? In spite of all his greatness the holy man was simple and humble. His heart was filled with a deep sympathy for the corporal and spiritual ills of his children. He not only taught them to know God, but filled their hearts with desire to serve Him. And so strong was the faith and love that he planted in their hearts, that they have held fast to the Church through centuries of persecutions and hardships of every kind.

At the death of St. Patrick in the year 461 not all the pagans of the island were as yet converted; still it is to this great saint that the people of Ireland owe their strong and beautiful faith. Holiness and learning came to Ireland with St. Patrick and continue to this day.

During the sixth and seventh centuries the Church of Ireland reached its greatest strength and beauty. There were monasteries of men and women spread all over the country. The Irish convent schools were at this time the best in all Europe. From these monasteries and schools hundreds of missionaries went out to bring the faith to other nations. St. Columba became the apostle of Scotland. St. Columban preached in the forests of France and Germany. Others went to England, Italy, and other parts of the continent.

Although St. Patrick himself never preached anywhere else but in Ireland, many other nations owe their faith to him and to the monks who came from the great Irish monasteries.

Now answer these questions:

1. How long was St. Patrick a captive in Ireland?
2. How did he escape?
3. Why did he want to get back again?
4. To whom did he preach first? Why?
5. How did he use the shamrock to teach?
6. Why is Ireland called the Island of Saints?
7. What did he teach his flock in Ireland?
8. Why is St. Patrick the patron of Ireland?
9. Is Ireland the only country that owes its gift of faith to St. Patrick?
10. Did he go to preach in other countries?

* * *

To be pleasing to God, it is not necessary to do great things. It is the many little acts of love and kindness that count. There are hundreds of chances for acts of kindness that come your way every day. Do you make use of them?

Ask yourself:

What kind acts can you do:
In school?
On the playground?
At home?
When you are with your friends?
Now pick out some kind act you are going to do today.

Choose something you have been forgetting about, and do it as soon as you get a chance. Tonight before you go to bed ask yourself if you have done what you planned to do. If you have, talk to God about it, and tell Him how much you enjoyed doing it for Him. If you have not, tell God you are ashamed of yourself and try again tomorrow.

Things to do:

1. Here are the names of a few of the great Irish saints who came from the monasteries founded by St. Patrick. Read about them and tell the class what you can imitate in their lives: St. Brigid, St. Gall, St. Brendan.

2. On the map of Ireland find Armagh, where St. Patrick lived a great part of his life and also Saul, in Ulster, where he died and was buried.

3. St. Columba was the first missionary from Ireland to go out and preach in another country. Find in the story of his life what country he converted.

4. Write a little story about a kind act done by a boy or girl. Read the story to the class.

5. Play the part of the story of St. Patrick which tells how he used the shamrock.

6. Draw or cut out a shamrock and use it for the cover of a booklet. In the booklet write the prayer "The Shield of St. Patrick" (*Rosary Reader VI*, p. 309).

7. Study the little poem "Kindness is the Word" (*De La Salle Reader V*, p. 160).

8. From the Old Testament tell the story of Joseph's kindness to his brothers.

9. Give examples from the New Testament that show the kindness of Jesus to the people of Israel.

10. Memorize the Scripture text: "As long as you did it to one of these my least brethren, you did it to Me" (Matt. xxv. 40).

11. Learn the hymn "Hail, Glorious St. Patrick" (*St. Gregory Hymnal*).

12. Memorize the following: "And Jesus coming, spoke to them, saying: All power is given to Me in heaven and on earth.

"Going therefore, teach ye all nations; baptizing them in the name of the Father, and of the Son, and of the Holy Ghost.

"Teaching them to observe all things whatsoever I have commanded you: and behold I am with you all days, even to the consummation of the world" (Matt. xxviii. 18–20).

Can you answer these questions?

1. What sacrament did St. Patrick receive when he prepared himself to be a missionary?

2. By whom can this sacrament be received?

3. Who administers the sacrament?

4. What kind of mark does it leave on the soul?

5. What other sacraments leave such a mark?

6. Of what is the shamrock an emblem?

7. What great gift do the people of Ireland owe to St. Patrick?

8. When is this gift first given to the soul?

9. What other gifts are given at the same time?

10. What prayers do we say to receive an increase of these gifts?

11. Say the acts of faith, hope, and charity.

Good things to read:

"Kind Words," *De La Salle Reader V,* page 158.

"The Shamrock," *Ideal Reader V,* page 122.

"The Apostle of Ireland," *Ideal Reader V,* page 124.

"St. Brigid, Patroness of Ireland," *American Cardinal Reader V,* page 313.

"St. Patrick," *Corona Reader IV.*

31. St. Boniface

In a sacred grove at Geismar, in Germany, stood an immense oak, known as the "Tree of Thor." This tree was held in great honor by the pagan Germans, who believed that it was inhabited by the god Thor. One day a large crowd gathered around the Tree of Thor. The pagans had boasted that, although the God of the Christians was great, He had no power over the sacred oak. No one, they had said, would dare to touch it, for fear of being punished by the god himself.

And now there stood before this mighty tree the great bishop St. Boniface, ax in hand. With his band of newly converted Germans around him, he was ready to prove that the God of Christians was stronger than Thor. He raised his ax. The people looked on in silent awe. The first blow fell. Nothing happened. Then came blow after blow until the sacred oak crashed to the ground. The God of the Christians had gained another victory.

Just as Ireland claims St. Patrick as the Apostle of its people, so Germany owes the gift of faith to the great St. Boniface.

Boniface was born in England about the year 675. As a boy of 7 he was sent to a Benedictine monastery to study. Later he became a priest and took charge of a monastery school. But ever since his boyhood he had wanted to be a missionary. Therefore, before long, he went to Holland, where he hoped to convert the pagan tribes that had overrun the country and destroyed the

St. Boniface cut down the sacred oak of the pagan
Germans and gained another victory for Christ.

churches and homes of the Christians. His attempt failed, however, and he went to Rome to get the pope's blessing for his future work.

On his return Boniface went into Germany, where he spent the greater part of his life, converting the pagans in different parts of the country. Everywhere he went, he converted large numbers to Christianity, often at the risk of his own life. When the pope heard of his success, he called him to Rome and consecrated him a bishop. It is after he became bishop that we meet him at Geismar, cutting down the sacred oak and erecting out of its wood a little chapel in honor of St. Peter.

To make sure that his work would continue, St. Boniface founded a number of monasteries and everywhere ordained priests to carry on the work of instruction among the converts. St. Boniface was once more honored by the pope by being made archbishop and receiving the power to consecrate other bishops, to help him in the immense work before him. Then, because Germany could not yet give him the missionaries that he needed, he went to England for volunteers and found many great men and not a few women ready to respond to his call.

Among the women who came as missionaries to Germany, was St. Lioba, a cousin of St. Boniface. This courageous saint founded three monasteries for women who were to be trained for the work of teaching the newly converted Christians. So great were her labors for the Church, that she has been called "the Woman Apostle of Germany."

From his work among the German tribes, Boniface was called to bring union and order among the Christian Franks, who occupied most of the land which is now called France. It was a difficult task, but he succeeded in bringing the rulers of the country more closely together and in preserving the faith of the people.

We have seen the important work St. Boniface did for the Church in Germany. But with all his success, he never forgot Holland, the country to which he had gone first, and to which he hoped some day to return. And so we see him as an old man, setting out for Utrecht, to continue his missionary labors where he had begun them years before. Everywhere he went, he met with great success. Thousands of men, women, and children received baptism, and many churches rose in place of pagan altars.

A happy day was soon to dawn for the newly converted people. They were to receive the sacrament of confirmation shortly after Pentecost. St. Boniface himself awaited the day with joy. He spent the night before in prayer and reading. Suddenly, in the early morning, there was a great noise. A band of men was fast approaching. They were not peaceful men, for they carried lances and swords.

When the attendants of Boniface saw the intentions of the fierce pagans, they took up whatever they could find of weapons and went out to defend the saint. But Boniface begged them to put away their swords and not to fight for him. He had hardly spoken the words, when the murderers began their bloody work. In a short time it was all over. St. Boniface and 52 of his followers lay dead upon the ground. The good shepherd had given his life for his sheep. The brave soldier had gone to his Leader, Christ. It was in the year 754.

Now answer these questions:
1. Why was the Tree of Thor sacred to the Germans?
2. What did St. Boniface do to this tree?
3. Why did he cut it down?
4. In what country was Boniface born?
5. Where did he go to preach first?
6. Was he successful there?
7. Where did St. Boniface work for the Church the greater part of his life?
8. How was he honored by the pope?
9. Who was the cousin of St. Boniface?
10. Why did she go to Germany?
11. What did St. Boniface do for the Franks?
12. Where did he die?
13. How did he die?

* * *

Jesus once said that the good shepherd gives his life for his sheep. Find the story of the Good Shepherd in the New Testament and read it to the class. Talk about it. It tells of Jesus' great love for us. Try to understand how much Jesus loves you. Thank Him today and every day for loving you so much. Tell Him often, especially at Holy Communion, how much you love Him. Perhaps you would like to use the following ejaculation: "Jesus, my God, I love Thee above all things."

Things to do:

1. On the map find the places mentioned in today's lesson.
2. In the *Lives of the Saints* read about St. Lioba and her work in Germany.
3. Draw the "Tree of Thor" and the little chapel which was made of its wood.
4. Find the feasts of SS. Boniface and Lioba. Would the vestments for both be the same color?
5. Find a picture of the Good Shepherd and post it on the bulletin board.
6. In a few sentences write which part of our story you like best.
7. Find how old St. Boniface was when he died. How many years were there between his death and that of St. Patrick?
8. Memorize: "I am the good shepherd. The good shepherd giveth his life for his sheep" (John x. 11).
9. The second Sunday after Easter is called "Good Shepherd Sunday." If you have a missal, look for the Mass of that day and see whether you can tell why it is so called.
10. Learn a hymn in honor of the Good Shepherd, such as "Loving Shepherd of Thy Sheep" (*St. Gregory Hymnal*).

Can you answer these questions?

1. What is confirmation?
2. How often may this sacrament be received?
3. Who gives this sacrament?
4. How must this sacrament be received?
5. How can a "lost sheep" return to God again?
6. How often does God forgive us our sins?
7. What attribute of God does that show?

8. What part of the "Our Father" tells us that we should also forgive others as God forgives us?

9. How did Jesus show His greatest love for us?

10. Why did He die for us?

11. Why could we not go to heaven unless He redeemed us?

12. What sin did we inherit from Adam and Eve?

Good things to read:

"The Good Shepherd," *Ideal Reader V*, page 41.

"For God and Country," *Misericordia Reader V*, page 102.

"Moni and His Goats," *Misericordia Reader V*, page 348.

"The Conversion of the Anglo-Saxons," *Shields Reader V*, page 205.

Psalm XXII, *American Reader V*, page 35.

32. St. Francis Xavier

One of the five young men who knelt with St. Ignatius Loyola in the Chapel of Our Lady to bind himself forever to the service of God, was Francis Xavier, a young nobleman. Francis, who was born in 1506 in the Castle Xavier in Spain, had always been ambitious. He wanted to do something great in the world, something that would make his name shine brighter than any other for the honor of Spain and the house of Xavier.

And all the while God must have smiled and thought as He once did of the proud Saul, "I shall show him how much he will have to suffer for My name's sake." Francis met St. Ignatius Loyola, as we know, and as a member of the Society of Jesus, dedicated himself heart and soul to the work of God and His Church.

He had reason, now, to be more ambitious than ever. For what was the honor of Spain or the house of Xavier to the honor of God? Oh, he would go and win souls,

St. Francis Xavier.

thousands of them, for his Captain, Christ! He could hardly wait to begin his mission. And St. Ignatius, knowing how the noble heart of this young disciple burned within him, sent him to far-away India, where millions of souls were living in paganism and sin.

Francis traveled by boat for a year and a month before he reached the port of Goa on the west coast of India. Goa was a large city supposed to be inhabited by Catholic Portuguese. But soon Francis found that these people were almost worse than the pagans. Here was work for him to do. He lost no time in preaching penance and forgiveness. In five months he had brought the entire city of 200,000 inhabitants back to the Church and the sacraments.

From Goa he went farther into the country. He would walk along ringing a bell until the children followed him. Then he would sit down and talk to them about God. The children ran home and told their parents what they had heard, and soon the older people came also. Thousands upon thousands of pagans received baptism within a few months. Churches rose everywhere, but they were hardly finished when they became too small. It seemed as though the time of the Apostles had again returned.

Sometimes it happened, however, that miracles were necessary to show the people the power of God. Francis raised a dead man to life, cured the sick, and saved a vessel from shipwreck. One time a large troop of soldiers came to kill him and the Christians. Francis took his cross in his hand and went out to meet them:

"In the name of the Living God, I command you to return," he called, and they turned and fled.

At times Francis was so tired after preaching and working all day, that he could hardly move. And yet his

heart was filled with so much joy that sometimes he had
to pray:

"My God, do not keep on. I cannot bear more joy."

Three hours of sleep is all he usually allowed himself.
The rest of the time he spent in prayer and work. In
seven years he had converted whole kingdoms and nations in the East Indies. Then he went to Japan, where
he preached the gospel for two and a half years.

The story is related that once the pagan Japanese
priests asked him to explain the Christian religion to
them.

"We shall put him to shame before all the people,"
they said among themselves.

But Francis spoke so beautifully, that at last they
had no more to say. They let him go on preaching for
several hours. Then the chief priest rose from his throne
and, kneeling at the feet of Francis, said:

"The people are being deceived by our religion, which
is full of idolatry and fables. Your religion is truly
divine."

The grace of God touched the hearts of the people
and five hundred asked at once for baptism.

Across the sea from Japan lay the immense country
of China. The heart of Francis, not satisfied with the
lands already won for Christ, longed to go there to
preach the gospel to the Chinese also. On the way he
became ill. From the lonely island of Sanzian, on which
he lay dying, he could see the coast of China. But like
Moses, he was not allowed to enter the land which he

longed to convert. He died alone in a poor hut. It was in the year 1552.

Francis was far away from all the glory he had dreamed of in his youth. And yet, like the glorious Apostle Paul himself, he is honored by the Church as one of the greatest missionaries of all times. He must have gained a million souls for God. What greater fame could he have won for the house of Xavier, for Spain, for his Order, and for his Church?

Now answer these questions:
1. What was the ambition of the young Francis Xavier?
2. What made him change his mind?
3. Where was he sent?
4. How long was he on his way?
5. How many people did he convert in Goa?
6. How did he get the pagan children and their parent to listen to him?
7. What are some of the miracles Francis performed?
8. Where did he go from India?
9. What did the chief priest say to Francis after he heard the saint preach?
10. Where did Francis want to go from Japan?
11. Did he get there?
12. To what great missionary is he compared?

*　*　*

Do you not long to do brave deeds for God when you read about the heroic work of St. Francis Xavier? A hero is brave not only in words but also in deeds. It is easy to say we are going to do big things when we grow older. Courage does not come in a day. We must be brave now and practice bravery

every day, if we wish to do great things some day for God
and our country.

Here are a few selections which will help you to think and
act courageously. Read them over, think about them, and
talk about them. Then ask yourself whether you also practice
them in your life:

One cannot always be born a hero, but one can always
be a man.

There is no finer courage than that which makes a person
say, "That is not right and I will not do it."

I must have courage to control not only what I do but
also what I think.

It takes courage to hold on:

To your tongue, when you are about to say an unkind word.

To your hand, when you are about to do an unkind act.

To your heart, when bad companions ask you to join them.

To your purity, when evil thoughts tempt you.

To your foot, when you are about to go where you should
not.

To the truth, when others will laugh at you.

To your temper, when you are excited and angry.

Things to do:

1. If you do not remember, read that part of the life of
St. Ignatius Loyola which tells about Francis Xavier.

2. On the map find Rome and from there show the route
St. Francis Xavier had to take by water to get to Goa on
the west coast of India. There was no Suez Canal at that time
and no way to get through the Mediterranean Sea to the
Indian Ocean. Can you see why it took St. Francis so long
to get to India?

3. Find Japan and China on the map.

4. Find the Feast of St. Francis Xavier.

5. Tell in what way St. Francis Xavier was like St. Paul; like Moses.

6. St. Francis Xavier died at the time when the Church was having a great Council. Can you find what Council that was?

Can you answer these questions?

1. What words from Holy Scripture made Francis Xavier become a poor missionary?

2. What do they mean?

3. What is idolatry?

4. What commandment forbids idolatry?

5. What is a miracle?

6. Does God still work miracles?

7. Have you heard or read about miracles that happened lately?

8. Can you explain the words, "Blessed is he that does not see and yet believes"?

Good things to read:

"Heroes," *Ideal Reader V*, page 129.

"The Little Drummer," *Misericordia Reader V*, page 116.

"Going, Going, Gone!" *De La Salle Reader V*, page 140.

"Harry's Contribution," *Ideal Reader V*, page 166.

MY GOD, I LOVE THEE

St. Francis Xavier

My God, I love Thee! not because
  I hope for heaven thereby;
Nor because those who love Thee not
  Must burn eternally.

Thus, O my Jesus, Thou didst me
  Upon the cross embrace!
For me didst bear the nails and spear
  And manifold disgrace.

And griefs and torments numberless
  And sweat of agony,
Yea, death itself — and all for one
  That was Thy enemy.

Then why, O blessed Jesus Christ,
  Should I not love Thee well!
Not for the hope of winning heaven
  Nor of escaping hell!

Not with the hope of gaining aught,
  Not seeking a reward;
But as Thyself hast lov'd me
  O everlasting Lord!

E'en so I love Thee and will love
  And in Thy praise will sing —
Solely because Thou art my God
  And my eternal King!
      — From the Latin by Edward Caswell.

33. Modern Missionaries

So far we have been following the history of the Church mostly in Europe. Perhaps you have wondered why. It was in Europe that the Faith spread during and especially after the time of the Apostles. Rome became the center of Christianity and has remained so always. You will remember, too, that America was not discovered until 1492. That means that no one on the continent of Europe knew until then that there was land to the west of the Atlantic Ocean.

If you will look into your American History, you will find that Columbus had several Franciscan Fathers with him on his ships, and that the first thing he did when he found the New World was to plant a cross on the new soil. That was the spirit of the Middle Ages. Everybody was Catholic. And while men were fond of fighting and were not always good, they thought and felt and spoke as Catholics wherever they went. Those who were good were always concerned about the glory of God and the salvation of souls.

When the New World was discovered, missionaries followed quickly to gain souls for Christ, just as St. Francis Xavier was doing in the East. The first missionaries to come to America were Franciscans, Dominicans, and Carmelites. They were followed shortly after by the Jesuits. They began at once with their work of saving souls, and in less than eighty years there were splendid

Christian communities in the West Indies, Mexico, Florida, Central America, and South America.

Just as centuries before, the missionaries had to teach the barbarians in Europe many things besides their religion, so in America they had to show them how to cultivate the land and to build homes of their own. A missionary had to know how to do many things. He had to be cook, gardener, doctor, nurse, shoemaker, tailor, carpenter, and mason all in one. But most of all, he had to have much love and patience. Sometimes it would happen, for example, that young Indians were sent out with a plow and a pair of oxen, to cultivate the field. Once in a while, when they did not return, the good missionary would find that they had killed the oxen and used the wooden plow to kindle a fire for roasting the meat. Then they had sat down and eaten and eaten day and night until they could not move.

But they learned their lesson in the end and became model Christians. Their little parishes were like a paradise on earth. All the Indians came together for morning and night prayers, and they lived such simple, upright lives, that a mortal sin was seldom committed by anyone.

The explorers, however, were generally greedy men who wanted nothing so much as gold. And so it happened that the Indians and the missionaries alike were often mistreated, their villages destroyed, and the people sold as slaves. We can imagine how the hearts of the priests bled for their poor children and how the

Indians became more shy than before, fled into mountains and forests, and came to mistrust and hate the
white men.

Among those who worked for the missions, especially
of Central and South America, were great saints whose
wonderful example was the cause of many conversions.

St. Louis Bertrand (1526–1581) was a Dominican
monk of Spain. He embarked for America in 1562 and
landed in New Granada. During the eight years in which
he worked among the natives, he baptized more than
25,000 pagans along the coast of Columbia and Panama.

St. Peter Claver (1580–1654) was a Spanish Jesuit.
He was ordained priest in New Granada and then sent
to Cartagena where he worked the rest of his life among
the Negro slaves. He was their apostle, father, doctor,
and friend. No matter how tired he was, when he heard
that a fresh shipload of slaves had come in, he went at
once to care for them in body and soul. Three hundred
thousand Negro slaves were baptized by him. He is
known as the Apostle of the Negroes.

St. Francis Solanus (1549–1610) was a Franciscan of
Andalusia. In 1589 he sailed for South America to
spread the faith. On the same ship with him were six
hundred Negro slaves. Some distance from the shore the
ship struck the rocks. There was only one lifeboat into
which the captain put the principal passengers. When he
asked Francis Solanus to go with them, the saint answered:

"Sir, you have done your duty; now I shall do mine.
I shall stay here."

Then he went to help those who remained on the ship with him. He prayed with them, instructed them, and baptized them. The ship was slowly sinking, and the passengers trembled with fear. Francis alone was not afraid. He trusted in God. At last, after three terrible days, the captain came back with another boat and saved them.

Francis worked among the Indians of Peru for 27 years and also among the Spaniards of Lima and Truxillo.

Lima was at that time a wicked city. Francis preached everywhere; in the streets, in public theaters, in gambling dens. With his cross in his hand, he frightened the sinful people by his terrible words of warning. At last he converted the whole city.

St. Turibius (1538–1606) was a Spanish nobleman. Already as a little boy he loved the Blessed Virgin dearly and said the rosary in her honor every day. As a school boy he would give away his food to help the starving poor. That was a wonderful preparation for the life of a missionary. No wonder he was found worthy, later in his life, to become archbishop of Lima, Peru. It was his duty to visit his bishops and priests and to watch over them and their parishes. He traveled 50,000 miles, and every place he went, he taught, baptized, and confirmed the natives. He also founded the first seminary in America.

These missionaries all worked in Central or South America, as we have seen. The North American missions were started later. We shall read about them in another lesson.

206 THE VINE AND THE BRANCHES

Now answer these questions:

1. When did the people of Europe find out that there was land west of the Atlantic Ocean?

2. What was the first thing Columbus did when he found the new land?

3. What things did a missionary have to know in those days?

4. Why did the Indians go back into the forests and hate the white men?

5. By what name is St. Peter Claver known?

6. What saint converted the wicked city of Lima?

7. How was St. Turibius prepared to become a missionary?

*   *   *

We are surprised when we read about the wonderful work of the early American missionaries. We are still more surprised when we remember that although many were from wealthy homes, they were prepared to help themselves in hundreds of different ways when they came to the missions.

Would you like to be of service to God or your country or your family when you grow older? Then you must learn to become useful while you are young; for the more things you know and the more you can do, the better you will be prepared to serve.

Ask yourself:

Am I useful at home?

Do I try to learn something new every day?

Do I ask other people to do for me what I can just as well do for myself?

Do I let my mother and sisters wait on me when I could easily wait on myself?

Do I help others when I can?

What can I do to make myself useful in school?

Do I prepare myself to become useful to God by learning all I can about my religion?

How can I be useful in my parish?

What have I learned today?

What would you do?

1. Don and you go out for a long hike. Don falls and cuts his wrist. He is frightened and does not know what to do. What can you do for him?

2. You and grandmother are home alone. Suddenly grandmother becomes very ill. What can you do for her?

3. Your little brother has some homework to do. He tells you that if you do it for him, he will wipe the dishes for you. How can you be most useful to your little brother?

4. Larry is in trouble. He has been in with a gang of boys who steal and do other bad things. He does not feel right about it and asks you for advice. Tell how you can be useful to Larry.

5. Ella's clothing catches fire. How could you make yourself useful to her?

6. Jack is alone in the school basement. He hears water rushing, becomes frightened and runs to his room without saying anything. What would you do?

7. Mother asks you to take care of the baby while she goes to town. She will not be back for a few hours. Shortly after mother has left, the baby begins to choke and scream. There seems to be something wrong. What could you do?

8. When you get home from school one day, mother has such a bad headache that she is not able to be up. What can you do to make yourself useful?

Things to do:

1. Find a picture of the landing of Columbus and write a story about it.

2. In your history read the story of the discovery of America and find out where Columbus first landed. Read also the story of Pizarro, the conqueror of Peru.

3. Locate on the map the different cities and countries mentioned in this lesson.

4. Do you know what a seminary is? Find out which is the nearest seminary to your city.

5. St. Rose of Lima was the first American saint. She was born during the time of St. Turibius. Find out more about her life.

6. The people of Lima were as wicked as those of Sodom and Gomorrha in the Old Testament. Tell the story of the punishment of Sodom and Gomorrha.

Can you answer these questions?

1. What sins did the explorers commit against the Indians?

2. What does the seventh commandment forbid?

3. What works of mercy did the missionaries perform?

4. What reasons did St. Francis Solanus have to trust in God?

5. Against what commandment does a person sin who gives way to impure thoughts and actions?

6. What does this commandment forbid?

7. How can you keep yourself pure in thoughts, words, and actions?

8. Against what commandment do they sin who do not speak the truth?

9. Against what commandment is anger?

Good things to read:

"Columbus," *Marywood Reader V*, page 43.

"Columbus at the Court of Spain," *Catholic Youth Reader V*, page 71.

A Game With the Saints

Twenty points is a perfect score.

1. A saint that reminds us of the shamrock. . . . .
2. The first American saint. . . . .
3. The Apostle of Germany. . . . .
4. The pope who died in exile because he had loved justice and hated evil. . . . .
5. An archbishop who traveled 50,000 miles to teach and convert the natives of South America. . . . .
6. The Little Poor Man of Assisi. . . . .
7. The father of the Blessed Virgin. . . . .
8. The Apostle of India. . . . .
9. The saint whose monks wear a white habit. . . . .
10. The saint who wrote the *O Salutaris* and the *Tantum Ergo.* . . . .
11. The Apostle of the Negroes. . . . .
12. The officer who became a saint by reading the *Lives of the Saints.* . . . .
13. The saint who wrote the *Memorare.* . . . .
14. The grandmother of our Lord. . . . .
15. The saint who remained on a sinking ship with the Negro slaves. . . . .
16. The teacher of St. Thomas Aquinas. . . . .
17. The founder of the Brothers of the Christians Schools. . . . .
18. The woman apostle of Germany. . . . .
19. The saint who converted 25,000 pagans in Columbia and Panama. . . . .
20. The saint who converted Scotland. . . . .

UNIT X

The Church as a Teacher

We have read how the Church sent out missionaries to all countries to teach men the truths of the Catholic religion. But who gave her the right to teach others? How can we be sure that the Church always teaches the truth? And when there are questions about matters of faith, how do we know that the Church decides correctly? Before Jesus ascended into heaven, He said to His Apostles: "Going, therefore, teach ye all nations ... and behold I am with you all days, even to the consummation of the world." With these words He gave the Church the right to teach and also the promise that He would be with her so that she cannot make a mistake. We shall see in the next lessons how the Church makes use of the right to teach her children the truths of religion; also, how the Blessed Mother herself at one time helped to show that the teachings of the Church are true.

34. The Vatican Council

In St. Peter's Church in Rome, the Vatican Council was coming to a close. It was the eighteenth of July in the year 1870. A solemn announcement was about to be made by Pope Pius IX in the presence of 535 bishops. The Holy Father arose and told those present what had been decided in the past seven months by the Council. The most important truths were the following:

"St. Peter was made head of the Church by Christ. The office which was given to St. Peter is still the same. The Pope takes the place of St. Peter. He is infallible when, as Chief Shepherd and Teacher of the whole Church, he speaks to the faithful in matters of faith or morals. All Christians must obey him. If anyone does not believe this truth, he is excommunicated from the Church."

When the Holy Father had finished this important announcement, a shout of joy went up in the large cathedral. Then from grateful hearts rang out that great Catholic hymn, "Te Deum."

But why were people so glad? Had not good Catholics always believed that the pope is infallible? Yes, the Church had always taught the truths which the Council declared, and until late years no one had denied them. But, since the time of the Great Revolution things had

The bishops gathering for a session of the
Vatican Council.

changed. The Protestants cut themselves off, as we know, from the true Vine. They would not obey the pope. Finally they said that he had no right to tell them what they must believe. It was time for the Church to declare before all the world what her children must believe, in order to remain living branches of the true Vine. There was no longer an excuse for any of them to say that the Church had never declared this teaching to be a dogma; that is, a truth which must be believed by all. "The pope," the Council declared, "is infallible." That means that he cannot make a mistake when he teaches something about our religion which we must believe or which we must do in order to be saved. From now on all people had to make a choice. Either they had to obey the pope and believe the doctrines which he teaches, or they would be excommunicated.

Sixteen years before, the same pope had made another solemn announcement. After writing to all the bishops of the world to ask what they thought, he declared: "Mary, the Mother of God is immaculate. She was never stained by original sin." To all Catholics who look upon the Mother of God as their own Mother, this truth was a great joy. They had always believed that God's Mother was never touched by sin, and now the pope had spoken and had declared their belief to be true.

Four years after the pope had declared Mary to be immaculate, the Blessed Virgin herself appeared to a dear little French girl named Bernadette and said to her: "I am the Immaculate Conception," which means that she was conceived without original sin. It seemed as if the Mother of God had wanted to show that we cannot make a mistake when we believe the teachings of the pope.

Now answer these questions:

1. How many bishops were at the Vatican Council?
2. What pope was at the head?
3. What did the Council decide about the pope when he teaches what we must believe and do in order to be saved?
4. What hymn of praise was sung after the pope had spoken?
5. What did Protestants say about the pope?
6. What other dogma did the pope declare sixteen years before?
7. To whom did Mary appear four years later?
8. What did she say to the little French girl?

*　　*　　*

Many times non-Catholics tell Catholics that they are foolish to believe what the Church teaches or that the pope is infallible. Protestants believe in the Bible. Can you use any of the following texts to answer them?

"He that heareth you, heareth Me; and he that despiseth you, despiseth Me" (Luke x. 16).

"Behold, I am with you all days, even to the consummation of the world" (Matt. xxviii. 20).

"Thou art Peter; and upon this rock I will build My Church, and the gates of hell shall not prevail against it" (Matt. xvi. 18).

"Feed My lambs, feed My sheep" (John xxi. 16, 17).

"Going, therefore, teach ye all nations" (Matt. xxviii. 19).

"I am the Vine, you are the branches" (John xv. 5).

"The Paraclete, the Holy Ghost, whom the Father will send in My name, He will teach you all things, and bring all things to your mind, whatsoever I shall have said to you" (John xiv. 26).

"Amen, I say to you, whatsoever you shall bind upon earth, shall be bound also in heaven; and whatsoever you shall loose upon earth, shall be loosed also in heaven" (Matt. xviii. 18).

Look for these quotations in the Bible.

Can you answer these questions?

1. Who gave the Church authority to teach?
2. Can the Church teach error? Why or why not?
3. Must a Catholic believe what the pope says about anything?
4. By whom was the Church founded?
5. How long will the Church last?
6. Who were the first bishops of the Church?
7. Who was at their head?
8. What is a dogma?
9. Where is the Catholic Church to be found?
10. Who helped to spread the Catholic Church over the world?

35. I Am the Immaculate Conception

It was a cold, dark Thursday in the month of February in 1858. Bernadette Soubirous, a little French girl of 14, was on her way to the hills outside of Lourdes to gather firewood. With her were Toinette, her younger sister, and Jeanne, a little neighbor. For a time the children walked along the bank of the River Gave and then over a meadow, where a mill stream crossed their path. The two younger girls took off their wooden shoes and waded over. Bernadette, however, was afraid of the cold water, for she had never been strong and feared she would become ill. Toinette and Jeanne went on alone and poor little Bernadette was left behind, not knowing what to do. At first she tried throwing large stones into the water so that she might step on them, but it was of no use. Then she decided to take off her shoes and stockings and wade across as the others had done.

Suddenly she heard a great noise, as if a storm were coming. She looked to the right and to the left, but nothing moved. Thinking that she might have been mistaken, she continued to take off her stockings. The noise came again. Then she jumped up frightened, and stood still. On the other side of the water rose a high rocky wall in which was a cave or grotto. As she looked over at this grotto, a golden cloud seemed to be rising from it; then a young and beautiful Lady came out and stood in an opening on one of the rocks. She wore a shimmering white gown with a blue girdle. On her head was a flowing white veil and on each of her bare feet a golden rose.

Bernadette rubbed her eyes, shut and opened them again. The Lady was still there; she was smiling as if to tell the girl that she is not dreaming. What was Bernadette to do? She was not a bright child. She had never learned to read or write, and just now when she was preparing for her First Holy Communion, she found it very hard even to learn her catechism. But she knew how to pray the rosary and always carried one with her. She pulled out her beads and knelt down. The beautiful Lady on the rock nodded and took her own rosary of pure white beads which she carried on her right arm.

With her eyes on the lovely vision before her, Bernadette prayed as she had never prayed before. And whenever she said the "Glory be to the Father" at the end of each decade, the Lady said the prayer along with her.

When the rosary was said, the Lady went back into the grotto and the golden cloud disappeared. Just then the two younger girls came back and called Bernadette to help them.

"Did you see anything in the grotto?" Bernadette asked them.

"No," they answered, "Why do you ask?"

"Never mind," said Bernadette, "It does not matter."

At home Bernadette told her mother what had happened.

"You have imagined that," said her mother. "You must not go there again."

Bernadette knew that she had really seen the sweet, lovely Lady, and she became very sad when her mother would not let her go to the grotto again.

But a few days later Bernadette's mother, seeing how sad her little girl was, told her she might go again to the grotto and take some of her little friends along. They took a bottle of holy water with them, "For," they said, "if it is an evil spirit, it will not like the holy water and will go away."

As soon as they had arrived at the grotto, Bernadette knelt down to pray, while the others watched eagerly to see what would happen. All of a sudden they heard her say:

"There she is, there she is!"

"Quick, throw some holy water at her," one of them said, handing her the bottle.

The lovely Lady nodded and smiled. The other little girls, who could see nothing but the bare stones, knelt down beside Bernadette. But she did not notice them any longer. Her face was lit up with joy. She seemed to be in another world.

When Bernadette saw the Lady the third time, she was asked to come back every day for two weeks. She agreed gladly; and many people came with her, although they could see nothing out of the ordinary except the wonderful look on the girl's face.

One day the beautiful Lady told Bernadette to take a drink from the spring. The girl looked around puzzled. There was no spring near. Then she began to dig in the earth with her fingers. All of a sudden water began to flow out of the ground.

Among the people who heard about Bernadette's vision were some who would not believe her story. "Who is the Lady," they asked, "and why does she not tell her name?"

Then came the twenty-fifth of March, the Feast of the Annunciation. Bernadette hurried to the grotto, and

"I am the Immaculate Conception."

even before she reached there, she saw the Lady waiting for her. Three times she asked:

"Will you not tell me your name, dear Lady?" At last the answer came!

"I am the Immaculate Conception."

It was the Blessed Mother. She told Bernadette that she wanted a church built on the spot where she appeared.

Two years later Bernadette went to live the life of a simple nun in a convent. Her only desire was to see our Lady in heaven. She died when she was only 35 years old, with the words on her lips, "Holy Mary, Mother of God." Since December 8, 1933, she is known as St. Bernadette of Lourdes. Her feast is celebrated on April 10.

In the place where our Lady appeared to little Bernadette, now stands a beautiful church to which thousands of pilgrims come from all over the world. Here many sick are cured in the waters of the spring, and many souls are brought back to God and His Blessed Mother.

Now answer these questions:

1. Who were the three little girls that went out to get firewood?

2. Why did Bernadette not cross the stream with the others?

3. What happened while she was alone?

4. How was the Lady dressed?

5. What did Bernadette's mother say when she told her about the beautiful Lady?

6. Why did the girls take holy water?

7. What did the Lady tell Bernadette to do during one of her other visits?

8. Who was the lovely Lady?

9. What do we find on the spot where our Lady appeared to Bernadette?

10. What often happens at the spring?

11. Where did Bernadette go some years after she had seen our Lady?

*   *   *

Mary was the purest of all women. Sin never touched her soul. She is our mother and our model. Like her we must be pure — in our thoughts, in our words, in our actions.

How to keep pure:

Go to the sacraments often.

Remember that God sees you always and knows your most secret thoughts.

Pray to Mary, the Mother of Purity, to keep you free from sin.

Keep away from bad companions, movies, and books.

Keep a strict watch over yourself. Do not look at evil, do not speak evil, do not listen to evil.

There are certain saints that are special patrons of purity. Here are some of them. Do you know anything about their lives?

St. Joseph, St. Aloysius, St. John the Evangelist, St. Stanislaus, St. Dorothy, St. Agnes, St. John Berchmans.

Things to do:

1. Find pictures of the saints mentioned and post them on the bulletin board.

2. Learn the prayer "My Queen, my Mother" and use it when you are tempted to sin.

3. Learn *O Sanctissima* or any hymn in honor of Mary Immaculate.

4. Dramatize the story of Bernadette.

5. Find a poem about Mary Immaculate.

6. Make a "Mary Book" by collecting all the beautiful poems about Mary that you can.

7. Find the Feast of the Annunciation and tell the story to the class.

8. Learn the following ejaculations in honor of Mary Immaculate: "O Mary conceived without sin, pray for us who have recourse to thee." "Blessed be the Holy and Immaculate Conception of the Blessed Virgin Mary."

9. Memorize any of the following quotations which you like. Be sure you think about them first so that you understand exactly what you are saying:

"Blessed are the clean of heart for they shall see God."

"He that loveth cleanness of heart shall have the King for his friend."

"Thou art the glory of Jerusalem, thou art the joy of Israel, thou art the honor of our people."

"Thou art all fair, O Mary, and there is no stain of original sin in thee."

"As the lily among the thorns, so is my beloved among the daughters."

Test Yourself

Can you answer these questions?

1. Should we believe anybody that tells us he has seen a vision?

2. Who do you think would have a right to decide such things?

3. Why do Catholics use holy water?

4. When should they use holy water?

5. Would it be right to believe that sacramentals always keep us from harm?

6. What is the sin from which Mary was free from the very beginning of her life?

7. What other sins was she free from?

8. What is the difference between original sin and actual sin?

9. What commandment tells us to be pure in thought, word, and deed?

10. What is forbidden by the sixth commandment?

Good things to read:

"The Virgin of Guadalupe," *Catholic Basic Reader V*, page 176.

"Blessed Bernadette," *Catholic Youth Reader*, page 8.

"The Names of Our Lady," *Ideal Reader V*, page 250.

"Hymn," *Rosary Reader V*, page 337.

"Hymn to the Virgin," *Shields Reader V*, page 236.

"Life of the Blessed Mother," *American Reader V*, page 4.

"Mary Immaculate," Eleanore C. Donnelly.

FIND AND WRITE OUT THE FOLLOWING SCRIPTURE TEXTS

1. Matt. xxviii. 19.
2. Luke x. 16.
3. John xv. 5.
4. John xx. 28.
5. Matt. iii. 17.
6. John xiv. 6.
7. Acts ii. 2–4.
8. Matt. xvi. 18.
9. John vi. 55.
10. Luke xxiii. 34.
11. Matt. v. 8.
12. Mark xiv. 22–24.
13. Matt. xix. 21.
14. John xx. 21.

15. Matt. xvi. 26.

UNIT XI

The Church, Mother of All People

When we look back over the history of the Church since its beginning, we find that she did for the people all that a real mother would do for her children. She not only taught them the way to heaven, but she also helped them to live in peace and happiness upon earth.

The early Christians were very thoughtful of one another. Those who were wealthy divided what they had with the poor. All lived together in love and harmony. They took care of the sick and buried martyrs as if they were their own sisters and brothers. No one was ever in want, for they felt that what God had given them should be shared with everybody. No wonder that the pagans said of them, "Behold how they love one another."

We have seen the Church as the mother of art and learning. We have heard her voice as a teacher of infallible truth. Now we shall learn how the Church shows herself also as the mother of the poor, the sick, and the oppressed.

36. Love Thy Neighbor as Thyself

Until a little over a hundred years ago, men did their work mostly in their own homes. The shoemaker made shoes in his own little workshop, where he had his own tools and his own way of making the shoes that were ordered from him. The cabinetmaker carved slowly and carefully at some beautiful piece of furniture. He felt that this was to be his work and that there would be no other like it in the world. So each man carried on his trade and lived a peaceful, quiet life at home with his own family. He could ask a fair price for his labor and if he was honest and a good workman, he was certain to earn enough to keep himself and his family in comfort.

All that is different now, we know. The invention of machinery, which began toward the end of the eighteenth century, made a great change in the lives of the people. Men, women, and even children went to work in factories. The factory owners often forgot the teachings of Christ and the Church. They thought only of money and how to get rich. Sometimes they treated the working people as if they had no rights; in fact, as if they were not human beings at all. If men wanted to earn a living, they had to work long hours in buildings that were often unsafe and unhealthy. And because they did not get enough pay, the whole family sometimes had to go to work; there was no more of the beautiful home life of former days.

Sorrow and suffering, misery and despair followed. Who was there, then, to take pity on the workingman and to speak for the poor and oppressed? The rich did not care, and the laborer had little or no rights.

But the teachings of the Church were still the same: "Thou shalt love thy neighbor as thyself" (Matt. xix. 19). "Thou shalt not steal." "Thou shalt not covet thy neighbor's goods." "Do unto others as you would have them do unto you." And the Church raised her voice and reminded rich and poor of their duty. She showed them that greed and injustice are sinful. She called on the employer to pay a just price for labor and on the laborer to be honest in his work. Nor did she stop there. She founded more societies to relieve the poor, built hospitals for the care of the sick, inspired pious men and women to spend their lives in looking after the needy families and in teaching them how to take care of themselves.

One pope especially saw the great need of his time and made it his work to concern himself about the poor and helpless. This was Pope Leo XIII who ruled the Church from 1878 to 1903. He was one of the most splendid rulers in the history of the Church. When he saw how unjustly the workingmen were being treated, he wrote a famous letter to all the Catholics in the world. Such a letter, when written by the pope for the instruction of all the children of the Church, is called an encyclical. The encyclicals which Leo XIII wrote in regard to the workingman and other important problems of the day, tell Catholics what kind of conduct is expected of them by the Church. His letter speaking of the rights and duties of laborer and employer has become especially famous all over the world. What he said in his letter has been used ever since by the bishops and other Catholic leaders, to settle the many questions about labor that still come up. You should know at least some of the points which the bishops have set down for a fair treatment of the workingman. They are really nothing new. The people have often heard these simple truths mentioned before. You have learned them in your catechism class. You have heard them often from the teachings of Christ Himself. How strange that so many people should forget. Read them over carefully and try to remember them all your life.

1. All creatures were created for the honor and glory of God. Therefore everything we do must be done for the glory of God. If we do all things for one purpose only, that is, for making money, we cannot be good Catholics or even Christians. Jesus said: "No man can serve two masters." By that He meant that we cannot make money our god and still remain children of the true God.

2. Man is made to the image of God. He is greater than all other creatures which were made for him. Therefore he must not be treated as a slave or a machine. He must be allowed to think and act for himself

as long as he does right. But, if he does not get enough wages, he cannot live like a free man. He becomes a slave of other men.

3. Man was not made for himself alone. He must think of other men also. He must work hand in hand with them. He must learn to obey just laws made for the good of all. Men are brothers. Christ is their elder brother and God is their father.

4. Men were created by God to live in families. The family holds people together. It is like the foundation of a building. Therefore, anything that helps to destroy the family cannot be good.

You see what a wise mother the Church is. She says to men: "You cannot be a hard-hearted business man who thinks of nothing else but making money, and at the same time be a follower of Christ. You cannot be unjust and then expect justice from God. You cannot refuse all love and kindness to others and expect God to love you. God has given you the things of this world, and you may use them to make yourself comfortable and happy. But you may never forget that you have an immortal soul and that you are made to know, love, and serve God."

Forty years after Pope Leo's encyclical appeared, our own Holy Father, Pope Pius XI, also sent out a famous encyclical in favor of the workingman. It is called "Forty Years After," because it begins with those words. In this letter the pope reminds the people of Pope Leo's words and again calls on them to work together for the good of all. He also mentions three remedies for the great evils of our times. They are: prayer, action, and sacrifice.

The Church knows that her children easily forget the laws of God and therefore she watches over them and sends great leaders, such as Pope Leo XIII, to instruct and guide them. She is truly a wonderful mother.

Now answer these questions:

1. Where did men do their work in past ages?
2. Why did each man do his work as beautifully as possible?
3. What made a great change in the lives of the people?
4. How were the working people often treated?
5. Why did whole families sometimes have to go to work?
6. Who raised her voice to speak for the poor and oppressed?
7. What else did she do for the poor and sick?
8. Which pope wrote a famous letter about the working people?
9. What are these letters called that are written by the pope for the instruction of all people?

*   *   *

We have just seen that if we expect justice and love from God, we ourselves must be just and loving toward others. The hard-hearted people who are not fair with their workingmen did not become so all of a sudden. They most probably committed many little acts of injustice in their lives. Perhaps they began when they were still young. Watch over yourself so that you do not become unfair in your dealings with others. We begin with small faults and sometimes end in great crimes.

Ask yourself:

Do I act as the following children?

1. Benny and Jack are playing a game of checkers. Benny cheats. His little brother saw him cheating. Benny says they are only playing a game and it really does not matter. What do you say?

2. Mayme cannot work her arithmetic problems. She asks the girl next door to do them for her. Is she fair to the teacher? to the class? to herself?

3. Ted is paid 15 cents a day for sweeping the store. Sometimes he finds money on the floor. He keeps it because, as he says, it does not belong to the storekeeper. Is he right?

4. Don promises his little brother Pat a nickel if he will carry in the wood for him. Afterwards Don gives Pat a tin coin that is no good. Is Don just?

5. Edna and Marie help Mrs. Leary with the dishes after a big party. Mrs. Leary gives Edna 50 cents for the two. They both did an equal share of work. Edna keeps 30 cents for herself and gives Marie twenty. Is she just?

6. Mother sends Fred to the store for some groceries. Fred keeps some of the change and pretends that the groceries cost more than they did. Mother is surprised that the grocer charges so much. To how many people is Fred unfair?

7. Viola breaks a vase in the living room. Afterwards she hears mother blame the maid. She does not say a word. To whom is she unjust?

8. Whenever the girls play a game Lorraine wants to take the lead. Otherwise she does not want to play along. Is she being fair to the rest?

9. Carol is sent to old Mrs. Deering with some fruit. Carol does not like to take things to this poor old lady and tells mother that Mrs. Deering has not been nice and does not even say "Thank you!" Mother sends no more fruit to the old lady.

If Carol said these things just to get out of taking food to Mrs. Deering, what fault has she committed?

10. Sister punishes Dolly for being late for school. Dolly tells mother that Sister treats her mean for no reason at all except that she does not like her. Mother believes Dolly, takes her out of the Catholic school and sends her to public school. In how many ways has Dolly done wrong?

11. Leo quarrels with the boy next door. They have a fight and Leo gets a black eye. Although he started the quarrel, he tells his father that he did not do a thing and that the neighbor beat him terribly. Leo's father quarrels with the neighbors and after that refuses to talk to them. In how many ways has Leo done wrong?

12. Every noon at school there are fifty bottles of milk given away to poor children. Len and his brother each get a bottle. Sometimes they sneak back in line to get another bottle. That means that a few children have to go without milk. Are Len and his brother fair?

13. Henry's father gives him 50 cents to go to the circus with his little brother. Henry pays for himself and sneaks his brother in without pay. Afterward they buy candy with the money they saved. Henry's big brother hears about the trick and says they were smart boys. What do you say?

14. Kenneth helps his father in the store. Whenever he waits on customers he gives them a little less than they pay for. He figures that he makes about 25 cents a day by weighing short. Suppose his father does not know anything about it, to how many people is Kenneth unfair?

Things to do:

1. Think of different ways in which you can help the poor.

2. Tell about some machinery that you think is a great invention.

3. Read the story of the Nuremberg Stove. Why did the

people love this stove so much? Do you think there were many stoves just like this one? Do you think it was made by machine just as our stoves are?

4. Study the text: "Seek ye therefore first the kingdom of God and His justice, and all these things shall be added unto you" (Matt. vi. 33).

5. Tell the story of Joseph who was unjustly sold by his brothers.

6. Find stories about men and women who spent their lives looking after the poor and sick.

7. Say the Eight Beatitudes and tell which of them speak of justice.

8. Can you make something all by yourself? Make some little thing like a booklet and do it as well as you can. You will find out how much fun it is to do a piece of work into which you have put your best efforts.

Now answer these questions:

1. Which is the greatest of all commandments?
2. Which commandment forbids us to steal?
3. Which commandment forbids us to covet our neighbor's goods?
4. What is envy?
5. Against which commandment is the sin of injustice?
6. What must they do who have taken goods unlawfully?
7. May people not try to make money?
8. Are all rich people unjust and hard-hearted?
9. Which commandment teaches us that we must adore but one God?
10. What is forbidden by this commandment?

Good things to read:

"The Golden Touch," *Cathedral Basic Reader V*, page 121.

"The Nuremberg Stove," *Cathedral Basic Reader V*, page 142.

"The Make-Believe Nun," *Cathedral Basic Reader V*, page 184.

"A Contented Workman," *De La Salle Reader V*, page 13.

"Two Laborers," *De La Salle Reader V*, page 15.

"The Missing Pages," *Ideal Reader V*, page 236.

"The King of the Golden River," *Shields Reader V*, page 109.

"The King of the Golden River," *American Reader V*, page 235.

"The Porcelain Stove," *American Reader V*, page 223.

37. St. Vincent, Father of the Poor

When Vincent de Paul was ordained in the year 1600, he was eager to begin his work as a priest of God among the poor people of France. But God allows strange things to happen sometimes to those who give themselves entirely to Him. One day when Vincent was on board a ship, he was captured by pirates and sold as a slave. He had to work hard from morning until night, but he never forgot that he was also a shepherd of souls. He often talked to the other slaves about God and showed them how to make their lives more pleasing to Him. After two years of slavery, he converted his master, who had lost his faith, and together they returned to France.

When Queen Margaret of France heard about Vincent, she gave him charge of distributing her alms. Nothing could have made him happier, for he loved especially to work among the poor. Later the king made Vincent inspector of the galley ships. Galley ships were great vessels rowed by chained criminals and slaves. The work was so hard that the men could only row a few hours at a time. Most of them died after a few years.

One day the inspector of the galley ships was missing. No one knew what had happened to him; no one had heard or seen him. A search was started for the saint, but for weeks he could not be found. Then, at last someone saw him. Vincent, the saint, was walking in line with the galley slaves and taking his place at the oars as he had done for weeks. When the governor of the city heard where Vincent was, he ran to the ship and on his knees loosened the chains from the saint's ankles. It had happened this way: A poor innocent man was condemned to work on the galley ships. That made his heart so hard, that he refused to speak or to work, no matter how terribly he was whipped. St. Vincent heard about the unfortunate slave and went to speak to him. By and by the poor man's heart softened, and he told Vincent his story. The saint felt so sorry for him that he put on the poor man's clothes, took his place as a slave, and sent the happy man home to his family.

Long, cruel wars had made many people of France heartless. Mothers would sometimes put their babies out in the streets to die. At night Vincent went out and picked up these poor children to bring them to the homes which he had built for them so that they might live and be happy, and learn to know and love God.

One night when he was walking along a dark street with one of these helpless babies wrapped in his cloak,

The men who had meant to rob St. Vincent de Paul
fell at his feet and begged his pardon.

some robbers rushed out at him. They thought he was carrying a treasure. But when they saw it was the holy Father Vincent, they fell at his feet and begged his pardon.

Because St. Vincent did so much for the poor, he often needed the help of the wealthy. Once he called all the rich ladies of Paris together and preached a sermon to them which touched them so deeply that they brought him their jewels as an offering for his works of charity. In order to give more help to his loved poor, he also founded the Lazarist Fathers and the Sisters of Charity, who were to assist him in his work of converting sinners and caring for the needy. But people were most easily converted when the saint himself, with his snow-white hair and eyes full of love, appeared and preached to them.

The work of St. Vincent did not end with the poor, however. Many of the leading people of Paris asked him to be their confessor. King Louis XIII of France died in the saint's arms. And yet, in spite of all the honor that was shown to him, Vincent was always gentle and humble. An angry man came up to him one day and struck him in the face. What did St. Vincent do?

"My brother," he said, "I beg your pardon if I have offended you."

The angry man was so taken by surprise, that he fell on his knees and begged the saint to forgive him.

St. Vincent died when he was 84 years old. Everybody

cried at the news, from the king on his throne down to the beggar in the poorest hut. But in heaven there must have been great joy when St. Vincent heard these blessed words: "What you have done to the least of My brethren, you have done to Me. Come into the joy of My Father."

Because St. Vincent showed himself a kind father to the poor, he is known as the patron of all charitable societies. The great society of St. Vincent de Paul was later named after him.

Now answer these questions:

1. What happened to St. Vincent de Paul shortly after he became a priest?
2. How long did he serve as a slave?
3. What work did he do for Queen Margaret?
4. What are galley slaves?
5. Why did St. Vincent work as a galley slave?
6. What did St. Vincent do for poor children?
7. Why did the rich ladies bring their jewels to him?
8. How did St. Vincent show that he was humble?
9. How old was St. Vincent when he died?

*   *   *

St. Vincent was a great apostle of charity. He was able to do so much good because he loved God and his neighbor with all his heart. It is not possible for us to do all that St. Vincent did. But there is much in his life and character that we can copy. Write out all the noble qualities you find in his life and then see which of them you would like to imitate. Here are a few to begin with. Add others to the list.

St. Vincent worked for souls even while he was a slave. He thought little of himself and a great deal of others. He loved the poor and worked for them all his life.

Things to do:

1. The greatest law which God has given us is: "Thou shalt love the Lord thy God, with thy whole heart, and with thy whole soul, and with thy whole mind." Do you think that St. Vincent kept this law? Tell the different ways in which he kept it. Memorize the law.

2. The Feast of St. Vincent is celebrated on the nineteenth of July. Find a picture of St. Vincent de Paul, and show it to the class. How is he represented?

3. Read about galley ships and write a short composition about them.

4. Draw a picture of a galley ship.

5. Dramatize a scene from the life of St. Vincent.

6. Tell the class what you like best in the story of St. Vincent and why.

7. Find a picture of a Sister of Charity (Medal Stories).

8. Do something for a poor child today for the love of God. Do not let anyone know about it except those whom you may have to ask for permission.

9. Tell what the people of your parish do for the poor.

Can you answer these questions?

1. Which is the greatest of all commandments?

2. Who is our neighbor?

3. Must we love only those who do good to us?

4. May people pretend to be poorer than they are in order to get more help?

5. Why should we share what we have with the poor?

Good things to read:

"Benito and His Posy," *Marywood Reader V,* page 296.

"St. Vincent de Paul," *Catholic Youth Reader V,* page 319.

"St. Charles Borromeo," *Catholic Youth Reader V,* page 146.

"Pierre's Little Song," *De La Salle Reader V,* page 32.

"The Angel of the Battlefield," *Misericordia Reader V,* page 107.

"Abou Ben Adhem and the Angel," *Shields Reader V,* page 146.

Test Yourself

Twenty points is a perfect score.

1. Jesus redeemed us by dying on the . . . .

2. After . . . . days He arose again from the dead.

3. The . . . . came down on the Apostles on Pentecost.

4. The Church has four marks. She is (*a*) . . . ., (*b*) . . . ., (*c*) . . . ., (*d*) . . . .

5. All over the world the Catholic . . . . teaches the same thing.

6. All Catholics obey the same visible head who is the . . . . in Rome.

7. Christ sent the Apostles out to teach all . . . .

8. The Catholic Church teaches the same thing that the . . . . taught after the descent of the Holy Ghost.

9. The Church received authority to teach from . . . .

10. When the Church teaches about faith and morals she is . . . ., that is, she cannot make a mistake.

11. Christ promised that the Church would last . . . .

12. The sacrament which gives the priest power to forgive sins is called ....

13. On the last day our bodies will rise from the ....

14. All those who die without mortal sin on their souls will go to ....

15. All the wicked shall be punished forever in ....

16. It is not enough to belong to the Church in order to be saved. We must also keep the ....

17. God said: "Thou shalt love thy .... as thyself."

UNIT XII

The Church, Mother of Saints

You have read much about the saints of God in the history of the Church. Perhaps you have noticed that people of all classes have been honored by that title. Among the saints there are bishops and priests, emperors and kings, doctors and lawyers, common laborers, and even wanderers. There are also great queens and mothers, nuns and servants, shepherdesses and young school children who have become saints.

Jesus calls each one of us to be holy. To strengthen us on our way through life, He gives us the sacraments. He, our Divine Model, is holy. The Church to which we belong is holy; therefore we, the children of the Church, the branches of the Vine, should also become holy.

In our next lesson we shall hear about other men and women who have become saints. Some of them, like the gentle St. Francis of Sales and the Little Flower, became holy by just doing the little things of life with a generous heart; others, like St. Teresa of Avila and the Jesuit martyrs, by heroic deeds done for the love of Christ. All alike, however, have been taught the ways of holiness by the Church. Truly, therefore, may the Church be called the Mother of Saints.

38. St. Francis of Sales

If we were to ask St. Francis of Sales to whom he owed his wonderful holiness, he would surely tell us he owed it to his mother. The first baby words she taught him to speak, were: "God and my mother love me very much." And later, when he understood what it means to commit a sin, she would repeat the words of the holy Queen Blanche: "My son, I would rather see you dead than have you commit a single mortal sin."

Francis was a lively little boy, with a temper that was easily aroused to anger. But he had made up his mind early in life, that he would overcome himself, for he wanted to become a saint. How long do you think it took him to learn the virtues which were hardest for him? It took him a long, long time; in fact, all his life. And what did he do to become a saint? He practiced the little virtues every day. It was not easy for him any more than it is for other boys who love fun and sometimes get into mischief. But he kept right on trying, and if he forgot himself, he thought of some way to make up the fault. Sometimes, for example, he would leave the room in anger and slam the door after him. Then he would remember that he must learn to be gentle. He would turn around, open the door quietly, excuse himself for being hasty, and then close the door again very softly. No wonder that Francis, in spite of his quick temper, became the saint of meekness and gentleness.

Nothing could make little Francis tell a lie, even when he knew he would receive a severe punishment by telling the truth. Neither could he see others punished. Sometimes he begged to take a whipping in place of someone else. Never was he happier than when he could give something to the poor; and when he had nothing more to give, he kept aside a part of his own meal for them. He could not bear to see anyone grieved or wronged. In a word, to make others happy was his greatest joy.

Francis and his parents lived in Annecy, France. When the boy grew up, he was sent to study at the university, first in Paris and later in Padua. At the age of 22 he received the degree of doctor of laws. Before returning home, he made a pilgrimage to Rome and to Loreto. He knew by this time, that God had called him to be a priest. But he was the eldest of the family, with a brilliant career before him. His father, the Count of Sales, was not willing to let him go. He tried in every way to make Francis change his mind. When he saw at last that nothing helped, however, he said: "Be happy, and may others find happiness through you."

At the time when Francis became a priest in the year 1593, a part of France had been torn away from the Church by heresy. The heretics were called Calvinists. Like other Protestants who had separated from the true Vine during the Great Revolution, they formed a religion of their own. Francis was sent to win them back to the faith. For four years he worked among them day and night. He was hated and persecuted and even threatened with death, but he continued his work without fear. In the end he had made 72,000 converts. How, do you think, was he able to win so many hearts for God? It

St. Francis of Sales.

was more by his wonderful gentleness than by his preaching.

In the year 1602 Francis of Sales was appointed Bishop of Geneva, a city in Switzerland, formerly belonging to France. His loving mother was still alive and had the church beautifully decorated for his consecration. She must have been very grateful to God for having given her such a good and holy son.

Even in his high office Francis always remained the same gentle, loving father to the rich and the poor, and especially to the children.

In the year 1604, Francis met a pious widow by the name of Jane Frances de Chantal. Together they founded a new Order for women, called the Visitation Order. This Order spread rapidly through France and other countries, also to the United States.

St. Francis did not go to pagan countries to preach, nor did he seem to do anything very different from what thousands of priests do today. And yet, he is known and loved throughout the world as the gentle and humble saint. He died in 1622; but even to this day the things he said and wrote help many souls to come closer to God.

Now answer these questions:
1. What were the first words St. Francis learned to speak?
2. What did Francis make up his mind to do?
3. How did Francis overcome his hasty temper?
4. What were some of the beautiful traits of his childhood?
5. Where did Francis study?
6. Why did the Count of Sales not want Francis to become a priest?
7. How long did Francis work among the heretics and how many did he convert?
8. Why was he able to convert so many people?

9. With whom did Francis found a new Order?
What was it called?

*   *   *

St. Francis became a saint by practicing the little virtues. Here are some of them. Look over the list and see whether you practice them. By practicing these little virtues you will make yourself loved by everyone.

Gentleness	Thoughtfulness	Helpfulness
Kindness	Cheerfulness	Christian Politeness

Talk these little virtues over with the class. Which of them are you going to practice especially today?

Here are a few sayings of St. Francis of Sales. Read them and memorize the one that you think will help you most:

"God the Father is the Father of mercy; God the Son is the Lamb; God the Holy Ghost is a Dove, that is, gentleness itself."

"We make little actions great by performing them with a great desire to please God."

"You will catch more flies with a spoonful of honey than with a hundred barrels of vinegar."

"Were there anything better or fairer on earth than gentleness, Jesus Christ would have taught it to us; and yet, He has given us only two lessons to learn of Him — meekness and humility of heart."

"No matter how little we say in anger, words may escape us that fill our hearts with bitterness for the day. But if we say nothing but a Hail Mary for patience, the storm passes by and we are pleasant and at peace."

Things to do:

1. Read the life of St. Frances de Chantal and find when her feast is celebrated.

2. Memorize the prayer "Jesus, meek and humble of heart, make our hearts like unto Thine," and say it when you are tempted to use angry words.

3. Find the cities mentioned in the story.

4. If you do not remember, find in the story of St. Louis the words which his mother, Queen Blanche, spoke to him.

5. Pick out all the virtues that Francis practiced as a child and tell which one you admire most.

6. Read the Eight Beatitudes and find the one which reminds you most of St. Francis.

7. Tell a story from the life of Christ that shows His meekness and gentleness.

8. Write out the little virtues mentioned in this lesson and next to each write the opposite fault.

9. Find pictures showing in practice each of the little virtues mentioned.

10. Find stories or poems about the little virtues mentioned.

11. Write a little story about a child showing one of these virtues.

12. Dramatize one of the stories you have read or written.

Can you answer these questions?

1. Against which commandment is the sin of anger?

2. What is the opposite virtue?

3. Against which commandment is lying?

4. What is the opposite virtue?

5. What are the sins against the eighth commandment?

Good things to read:

"The Patient Job," *Marywood Reader V*, page 95.

"The Little Dandelion Seed," *Marywood Reader V*, page 3.

"The Old Gentleman's Path," *Catholic Youth Reader V*, page 8.

St. Catherine of Alexandria.

St. Elizabeth of Hungary.

St. Rose of Lima.

St. Thérèse, the Little
Flower.

"A Lesson in Politeness," *Catholic Youth Reader V,* page 144.

"The Four Sunbeams," *Catholic Youth Reader V,* page 162.

39. Woman's Work in the Church

In the life of St. Francis of Sales we read that he owed his great desire to be a saint to his good mother. We remember, too, that St. Augustine was converted by the prayers of his holy mother Monica, and that St. Louis of France learned from his mother, Queen Blanche, to keep away from mortal sin.

When Jesus walked the earth, good women took care of His and the Apostles' needs; and when later the Apostles formed the new Christian communities, the women again helped in the care of the poor and needy and in doing other work for the Church. From those early days down to our own times, brave and holy women have done their full share for the Church, either by their good example or by their prayers and labors. As we read the story of the early martyrs, we find that wives and daughters gave up their lives for their faith as willingly as husbands, sons, and brothers. St. Cecilia, St. Agnes, St. Perpetua, St. Lucy, St. Dorothy, and St. Catherine are only a few of the well-known names of Christian martyrs.

St. Helena, the mother of Constantine, went to Jerusalem, we know, to find the true cross of Christ. The pagan Franks became Christian through the example and prayers of the Catholic queen, St. Clotilda, wife of Clovis, their king. When St. Boniface needed help in the conversion of the Germans, his cousin, St. Lioba, came from England with a band of women to assist him in his missionary work and to found with him three monasteries for women.

So in every age, women played an important part in spreading God's Church on earth, each in her own way: some, as we have seen, by performing great and heroic deeds, others by being faithful in the little duties of everyday life. We shall look at a few of these saints and learn how each carried on the work of God in a different way and how all became holy through their great love for Him.

St. Hildegard of Bingen was abbess in a Benedictine Order in Germany in the twelfth century, during the lifetime of St. Bernard. She was a woman of splendid education and great piety. Rich and poor came to her for help and instruction. Popes, emperors, bishops, and abbots wrote to her for advice. She knew a great deal about animal and plant life and also about medicine. Besides this she wrote poetry and composed musical hymns for use in church. She did, perhaps, as much good among the people of her time as the great St. Bernard himself.

St. Catherine of Siena lived toward the end of the Middle Ages. She became a member of the Third Order of St. Dominic and spent much of her time alone in prayer and works of penance. In 1374 a terrible plague broke out and she waited on the sick without a thought of her own health. Later, when war broke out between the Republic of Florence and the pope, she traveled from city to city, converting hardened sinners and begging the rebellious people to obey the pope. She went to Avignon in France, where the pope had been living as a captive of the king, and pleaded with him until he came back to Rome. She wrote letters to kings and queens, and to popes, cardinals, and bishops, to make peace in the Church. When peace was finally made, Catherine returned to her humble home in Siena. But soon trouble broke out again and she went once more to Rome to take up the cause of the pope. Day and night she wept and prayed for peace and unity in the Church. The troubles of the Holy Father seemed like her own. She wore herself out trying to win the people to support the pope and died an early death, being only 33 years old.

Up to the end of the fifteenth century all Orders had been founded by men. Now *St. Angela Merici* started a new Order of women known as the Ursulines. They promised to practice the spiritual and corporal works of mercy, to instruct children, especially poor girls whose parents could not afford to hire teachers, and also to care for the sick and prepare them for the Last Sacraments. The Order spread rapidly, first over Italy and then into France and Germany. The first Ursuline nuns came to the United States in 1727. They number nearly 7,000

Mother Elizabeth Ann Seton
Sisters of Charity of St. Vincent
de Paul.

Mother Alphonsa Lathrop
Dominican Sisters, Servants of
Relief for Incurable Cancer.

Mother D'Youville
Grey Nuns of Montreal.

Mother Caroline
School Sisters of Notre Dame.

members at this time. We can see from that number how great must be their work for the Church, especially in instructing children.

What St. Angela Merici started out to do, was a begin-

St. Angela Merici, foundress of the Ursulines, one of the great teaching Orders of the Church.

ning for the great number of Orders that have since sprung up in different countries to carry on the work of the Church. Heroic women have set out to found Orders wherever the Church most needed them. Some found the teaching of children the greatest need of their time, others saw that hospitals had to be founded. Some spent their time caring for the wounded on the battlefield, others in going into the homes of the poor and neglected.

Everywhere, in Europe and in the United States, in the jungles of Africa, in distant China and Japan, wherever the missionaries went to carry the Faith, noble women followed in their footsteps to do any kind of work for which they might be needed.

Not all Orders of women, however, give their time to spreading the Faith by external works of mercy. There are those who spend their lives in praying for the conversion of sinners and for God's blessing on the world. Such are called contemplative Orders; and it is in one of these that we find the little saint so dear to the hearts of children, the *Little Flower*. Hers was a hidden life, and yet so filled with the love of God, that the whole world has become better for having known her. She spent her short life on earth shedding a sweet perfume around her. She did all her little duties as well as she knew how and God was pleased with His Little Flower and made her a great saint. She lived almost in our own time. She was born in France in 1873 and died as a Carmelite nun in 1897. The Church honors her as a saint since 1925. Her feast is on the third of October.

Other saints have been called to do still other work. *St. Germaine* was a little shepherdess who became a saint by patiently bearing her hard life for the love of God. *St. Joan of Arc* was appointed by God to save France by leading the king's army to victory against the English. The great *St. Teresa of Avila* was chosen to bring the Carmelite Order back to its strict rules and to lead many souls to God by her writings. *Queen Elizabeth of Hungary* was a model wife and mother as well as a humble servant of the poor. *St. Zita* has taught young girls that they can become saints even while doing the hard work of a servant.

A look at the *Lives of the Saints* will show us many more names of women who, after the example of Mary, the Queen of Saints, have spent their lives for Christ. Their shining example should remind us that God often chooses the weak things of this world to do the work of the strong. With St. Teresa of Avila we, too, can say: "Teresa alone can do nothing; but Teresa and God can do everything."

Now answer these questions:

1. What did good women do for Jesus while He was still on earth?
2. Who were some of the well-known Christian martyrs?
3. By whose example and prayer was Clovis converted?
4. Why did popes and emperors come to St. Hildegard?
5. How did St. Catherine of Siena work for the Church?
6. What work did the Ursulines promise to do?
7. For what kind of work were different Orders founded?
8. What do the contemplative Orders do?
9. What kind of nun was the Little Flower?

10. How did she become a saint?

11. Who were some of the other saints mentioned?

*   *   *

God wants us all to become saints. To become a saint, it is not necessary to do great things, but only to do our duty every day as well as we can. Look over the saints mentioned in this lesson and see which one you would like to imitate. Point out one virtue that you can practice this week. At the end of each day ask yourself whether you have kept up your little practice.

Things to do:

1. Look back at the stories of St. Augustine and St. Louis and find how the mothers of these saints helped them to become holy.

2. Tell the class how St. Helena found the true cross.

3. Look for the life of St. Lucy and find of what she is patron.

4. Read the life of St. Dorothy and then write a play about it.

5. Find pictures of great women saints and put them up on the bulletin board.

6. Read the story of the Little Flower and tell what you like best about her.

7. How many different Orders of Sisters do you know? Ask your teacher to tell you about some of the great women in her Order.

8. Prepare a little program of songs, recitations, and stories about great women, and give it in honor of the teachers in your school.

9. Find Avignon in France. Ask your teacher to tell you how it happened that the pope was a prisoner there.

10. Bring to class pictures of Sisters working in the hospital,

on the battlefield, and in the classroom among the people of different nations.

11. Read the story of Joan of Arc. She is sometimes shown in the Cathedral of Rheims with the king. Write what you know about this cathedral.

12. Make a poster with one of the following sayings:

"After my death I will let fall a shower of roses." — *Little Flower.*

"All things pass away." — *St. Teresa of Avila.*

Do the duty that lies nearest you.

Blessed are the clean of heart for they shall see God.

Be faithful in little things.

13. Draw or cut out a picture for the story of one of the saints you have read.

14. Sing a hymn or learn a poem in honor of one of these saints.

Can you answer these questions?

1. On what day does the Church celebrate the Feast of All Saints?

2. What helps has God given us to gain heaven?

3. What is grace?

4. How many kinds of grace are there?

5. What virtues does sanctifying grace bring into our souls?

6. Make an act of faith, hope, and charity.

7. What is actual grace?

8. Is grace necessary for salvation?

9. The saints made good use of the graces God gave them. Could they have refused the grace of God?

Good things to read:

"The Little Flower," *Cathedral Basic Reader V*, page 282.

"The Maid of France," *Catholic Youth Reader V*, page 107.

"The Better Land," *Ideal Reader V*, page 264.

"Our Nuns," *American Cardinal Reader V*, page 13.
"The Childhood of St. Joan of Arc," *American Cardinal Reader V*, page 31.
"St. Ursula and Her Companions," *Misericordia Reader V*, page 42.
"Joan of Arc Crowns the King," *Shields Reader V*, page 283.

40. The Jesuit Martyrs of North America

Christmas Day on the coast of France. A tired traveler kneels in adoration in a little village church and pours out his thanks to the newborn King. He has had a long and weary journey across the sea, and now he is once more in his native land. Six years ago he had left home and country to work among the Indians of North America, expecting to lay down his life there. And here he was, back in France! No wonder his heart was glad.

A journey of five days brought him to the house of the Jesuits at Rennes. He knocked at the door and asked for the Superior.

"Father Superior cannot see you now," answered the porter; "he is getting ready to say Mass."

"Tell him," answered the traveler, "that a poor man from Canada would like to speak to him."

The superior came at once.

"You are from Canada?" he asked.

"Yes, Father."

"Do you know Father Jogues?"

"Yes, Father, very well."

"He was captured by the Iroquois Indians. Is he dead?"

"He is alive, Father. I am he."

We can imagine with what joy the people of France welcomed the holy Jesuit. Everybody wanted to see and hear him. Even the Queen of France asked him to come to the Court that she might speak to him.

After a short time spent with the Jesuit Fathers in France, Father Jogues went to Rome. It was only natural that he should long to kneel at the feet of the Holy Father, for was not the pope the head of that glorious Church for the spread of which Father Jogues was ready to lay down his life? And in Rome a happy surprise awaited him. During his stay among the Indians, he had been shamefully treated. Whenever anything had gone wrong, the "Blackrobes," as the missionaries were called, were blamed. At one time, when he was taken captive and cruelly tortured, the Indians chewed off and later burned off some of his fingers. Therefore, it was not possible for him to say Holy Mass, the greatest happiness a priest has on earth. But when the Holy Father saw his crippled hands, he said: "It is not fitting that Christ's martyr should not drink Christ's blood," and gave him permission to say Mass, in spite of the missing fingers.

Father Jogues had the heart of an apostle. He longed to go back to his dear Indians in the hope of gaining more souls for Christ. And so, after a few short months at home, we see him once more on his way to America.

The first Jesuit missionaries who were later honored by the Church as martyrs, came to Canada in 1625. They were Father John de Brébeuf and Gabriel Lalemant. They worked principally among the Hurons, a tribe that lived in that part of Canada just east of Lake Huron. It took years of hardship and sacrifices to reach the hearts of these ignorant and superstitious men. In 1636 Father Isaac Jogues came from France to join Father Brébeuf and the other Jesuits in their work of saving souls. For six years he labored among the savages in the country around the Great Lakes. He was the first Catholic priest to travel down into the United States as far as Manhattan Island.

In the year 1646 Father Jogues visited a village where Auriesville, New York, now stands. He wished to meet the Iroquois Indians, the greatest enemies of the Hurons, in order to make terms of peace with them. He was captured at Lake George, tortured, and finally put to death. With him were René Goupil, a lay brother, and John Lalande, a layman, who were both martyred about the same time with Father Jogues.

Two years after the death of Father Jogues, Fathers Brébeuf and Lalemant also became victims of the fierce Iroquois. To this list of glorious martyrs are added the names of three other Jesuits. They are Fathers Charles Garnier, Noel Chabanel, and Anthony Daniel, who gave up their lives as the others had done, so that the poor Indians, too, might become children of the Church and branches of the true Vine. They were all canonized on

The early missionaries in North America suffered
many hardships for Christ.

June 29, 1930. The Feast of the Jesuit Martyrs of North America is celebrated on September 29.

We know from the early history of the Church that the blood of the martyrs is the seed of Christianity. Shortly after the death of Father Jogues 3,000 Hurons were converted. The very ground which received the blood of the martyrs was the birthplace of the holy Indian girl, Catherine Tekawitha, known as the Lily of the Mohawks, whom the Church will some day perhaps honor as the first saint born in our own United States.

Now answer these questions:

1. Who was the man that knocked at the door of the Jesuits in Rennes?
2. Where did he come from?
3. What was the happy surprise that awaited Father Jogues in Rome?
4. Did Father Jogues remain in France?
5. What two Jesuit missionaries came to Canada in 1625?
6. Among what tribe did they work?
7. Who was the first Catholic priest to travel into the United States as far as Manhattan Island?
8. What day is the Feast of the Jesuit Martyrs celebrated?
9. Who is the Lily of the Mohawks?

*   *   *

The history of North America is full of stories of the heroic deeds and explorations of Catholic missionaries. The work still continues today in different parts of the country. Priests and Sisters of different Orders work for the bodies and the souls of the poor Indians who were once the proud owners of this glorious land of ours. Most of the missions where Indians are being taken care of, are very poor. Catholic mission societies send them food and clothing and perhaps toys for the children. Have you ever done anything for the Indian missions? Plan with your teacher and classmates to do something for a Catholic Indian mission.

Things to do:

1. On the map find the places mentioned in this lesson.

2. Have one of your classmates write for a copy of *The Indian Sentinel,* to the Bureau of Catholic Indian Missions, 2021 H Street, N.W., Washington, D. C. It will show your class what Catholic missionary priests and Sisters are doing for the Indians in North America.

3. Read the story of Father Marquette or another great missionary and tell the class about it.

4. Dramatize the arrival of Isaac Jogues in France.

5. In your history find the names of as many early missionaries as possible and write in what part of the country they worked.

6. Find pictures of the famous Franciscan missions in California. See what you can learn about them.

7. Write a little story about an Indian and a "Blackrobe."

8. Draw a picture for an Indian story.

9. In some of the readers you will find interesting stories about the early missionaries. Read some of them and tell the best one to the class.

10. Find some good Indian pictures and put them on the bulletin board.

11. Find out some of the superstitious beliefs of the Indians and see whether they will help you understand why it was hard to convert these people.

12. Find out whether there is any interesting Indian history connected with your church and tell the class about it if there is.

13. Read the story of Tekawitha, the Lily of the Mohawks, and tell the class something about her life.

14. Study the poem, "Knowest Thou Isaac Jogues."

Can you answer these questions?

1. Why could Father Jogues not say Mass without permission from the pope? If you do not know, ask your instructor about it.

2. What did the Holy Father mean by his words about Father Jogues?

3. What does it mean to be superstitious?

4. Against which commandment is this sin?

5. What other sins are against the same commandment?

6. Is it superstitious to wear a blessed medal?

7. What superstitious practices do you know?

Good things to read:

"Winning the New World for Christ," *Marywood Reader V,* pages 312 and 335.

"Father Marquette and the Indians," *Cathedral Basic Reader V,* page 161.

"The Coming of the Blackrobe Chief," *Cathedral Basic Reader V,* page 167.

"The Flaming Torch in the American Forest," *American Reader V,* page 87.

"The Oak of Monterey," *Rosary Reader IV,* page 76.

"Knowest Thou Isaac Jogues," *Rosary Reader IV,* page 255.

Test Yourself

Each of the following statements is answered by one of the words below. Number the words with the same number as the statement to which it belongs. Ten points is a perfect score.

1. The Isle of Saints.
2. A tree held sacred by the pagan Germans.
3. The country in which St. Boniface gave up his life.
4. The land which St. Francis Xavier longed to convert but never entered.
5. The city in which the first American saint was born.
6. The Council which declared the infallibility of the pope.
7. The title by which the Blessed Virgin called herself when she appeared to little Bernadette.
8. A letter which is written by the pope for the instruction of all Christians.
9. An Order of Sisters founded by St. Vincent de Paul.
10. The king who was converted by his Catholic queen.

Encyclical
Ireland
Clovis
Sisters of Charity
Lima

China
Tree of Thor
Holland
Vatican
Immaculate Conception

UNIT XIII

Other Leaders of the Church

All people may become saints, as we have seen. Priests and nuns are not the only ones who are called upon to do great things for God. The Church wants all of us to be apostles. We cannot all die for our faith, but we can live for it and help to defend and spread it.

More than ever the Church needs men and women to spread and defend the Faith. Our Holy Father, Pope Pius XI, has called on all Catholics to take part in Catholic Action. The Church needs you, too. Learn to know your faith well, therefore, that you may be ready, when your turn comes, to take your place among the leaders and apostles of the Catholic Church.

We shall now read about three men whose lives show us different ways in which we can work for God and the Church, even if we are not called to the priesthood or the religious life. These men loved their wonderful faith above everything else, and stood by it in spite of great difficulties.

41. Saint Thomas More

Let us imagine we are in a lovely English garden in Chelsea near the city of London. Two men are walking up and down the path enjoying a friendly chat. The taller and younger of the two has his arm around the neck of the older man and looks fondly at him as they talk. The one is the King of England, Henry VIII, the other Sir Thomas More, his chancellor. At the end of nearly an hour, the king takes his leave and Sir Thomas walks into his house.

"You are a happy man, Sir Thomas, to be such a favorite of the king," says his son-in-law.

"I find His Grace a very good lord, indeed," answers Sir Thomas, "but I tell you I have no reason to be proud; for if my head would win him a castle in France, it should not fail to go."

He meant to say that King Henry could not be trusted, for he would be willing to cut off people's heads for a very little excuse.

Both these men were soon to take an important part in the history of the Church: King Henry by tearing the entire country of England away from the true Vine and making himself head of the Church of England, and Sir Thomas More by losing his head in defense of the pope's rights.

It was at the time when Luther had spread his false teachings over Germany and other countries. Henry VIII and the people of England really had no desire to separate from the Church of Christ. The king even wrote a book in which he defended the Catholic faith and for which the pope gave him the title "Defender of the Faith."

But not many years later, in the year 1527, Henry wished to have a divorce from his first wife, Catherine, so that he could marry another woman whose name was Anne Boleyn. The Holy Father said it was not lawful for the king to put away his wife and marry again; and because Henry could not have his way, he separated from the pope and called himself the head of the Church of England. The bishops and priests of England were either bribed or forced to sign an oath in which they declared that they would look upon the king as the supreme head on earth of the Church of England.

Among the few men who refused to take the oath, was one bishop, John Fisher, and Sir Thomas More, whom we saw in the garden of his Chelsea home as the trusted friend of the king.

Thomas More was neither a priest nor a bishop, but the father of a family and one of the greatest scholars and statesmen of his time. He had held the highest offices in the kingdom, among them the position of chancellor, which means that he was the king's right-hand man. In his youth he studied law. He used to rise at two o'clock in the morning in order to find time for

Saint Thomas More, worshiping his heavenly King, bids the messengers of the King of England wait.

further study and for his prayers and many writings. Every day of his life, as long as it was possible, he heard Mass before he attended to any other business. One day the king sent for him while he was at Mass. Sir Thomas More wished to remain to the end of the Mass. The king sent a second and a third message, but the great statesman would not leave until the Mass was over. To those who called him and asked him to go at once to the king, he said:

"I am paying court to a greater and better Lord than Henry, and must perform that duty first."

As Henry was then still a good and God-fearing king, he was not offended at More's words.

We can well understand that a man of such deep piety and splendid character could not be bribed even by a king to do anything against his conscience. We can see, too, that the king would have wished, above all things, to have Thomas More on his side when he tried to get the pope to grant him a divorce. Perhaps King Henry thought of that when he made Sir Thomas More his chancellor. Perhaps he hoped Sir Thomas would approve of his second marriage if he honored him by this high office. But if that is what King Henry thought, he soon found out that he was mistaken.

For three years Sir Thomas More served the king faithfully, although he knew well what his position might cost him. When he saw, however, that he would have to side with the king against the Church or give up his office as chancellor, he resigned.

But Henry was not satisfied. He could not bear to think that so great and fearless a man as Sir Thomas should refuse to do his will. Sir Thomas was asked to sign the oath which nearly everyone in England had signed. He knew what it meant to refuse. He had to make a choice between life and death, between honor and shame. He made his choice bravely and fearlessly. He refused to sign the oath and was thrown into prison to await his trial.

Thomas More had been a good husband and father, a perfect statesman, and a loyal subject of his king. But never had the faith that was in him shone more brightly than when he was a prisoner in the tower of London. He was happy that he could now spend his time in closer union with God. He wrote and meditated and led a life of prayer and penance. He had always trained himself to make the best of everything and now that he was in prison he found nothing too hard. Whenever his wife or children visited him, he seemed to be in the best of spirits. Sir Thomas spoke to them cheerfully and told them that it made little difference after all whether a man died today or tomorrow. His only thought was to act according to his conscience, no matter what the cost.

At last, after an unfair trial, Sir Thomas More was condemned to death. When the sentence was passed, he said among other things: "I know well that the reason why you have condemned me is because I have never been willing to consent to the king's second marriage; but I hope in the Divine goodness and mercy, that, as

St. Paul and St. Stephen whom he persecuted, are now friends in paradise, so we, though differing in this world, shall be united in perfect charity in the other. I pray God to protect the king, and give him good counsel."

When Sir Thomas More went up to the scaffold for his execution, he asked all the people who stood around, to pray for him. "I suffer death," he said, "in and for the faith of the Catholic Church."

He knelt down and said the psalm *Miserere,* which had always been his favorite prayer. Then he blindfolded himself and placed his head upon the block. The executioner struck the fatal blow, and Sir Thomas joined the glorious ranks of those who have given their lives for their faith. He was canonized on May 19, 1935, at the same time with Bishop John Fisher, who was also beheaded for his loyalty to the Church.

Now answer these questions:

1. Who were the two men walking in the garden?
2. Why did Sir Thomas More say he had no reason to be proud?
3. What important part did Henry VIII play in the history of the Church?
4. What important part did Sir Thomas More play?
5. Did the English people wish to leave the Church?
6. What title did Henry receive from the pope? Why?
7. Why did Henry break away from the Church of Rome?
8. What bishop refused to take the oath?
9. What shows how much Thomas More thought of the Mass?
10. How long did Sir Thomas act as chancellor?

11. Why did he resign his office?
12. Why was Henry VIII not satisfied?
13. Why was Sir Thomas thrown into prison?
14. How did he die?

*   *   *

Sir Thomas More understood the meaning and the value of the Mass. That is why he attended the Holy Sacrifice every day. See how much you can learn about the Mass this week.

Ask yourself:

Do I love the Mass?
Do I understand what happens at Mass?
Do I try to attend Mass whenever possible?
Do I attend with attention and devotion?
Do I try to learn more about the Mass from day to day?
Do I follow the prayers of the Mass?

Things to do:

1. Dramatize a scene of Sir Thomas More's life.
2. Draw or cut out the vestments used at Mass.
3. Make a chart of the articles used at Mass.
4. Write a composition telling about the different colored vestments used at Mass and tell the meaning of the colors, when they are used, etc.
5. Write or tell the story of one of the sacrifices of the Old Testament and tell how it is like the Sacrifice of the Mass.
6. Say the words of St. Thomas, the Apostle, every day at elevation: "My Lord and my God."
7. Find a picture of the Last Supper and tell the story.
8. Memorize the words which our Lord spoke when He gave the Apostles His own Body and Blood at the Last Supper.

Can you answer these questions?

1. How often should one hear Mass?
2. What is the best way of hearing Mass?
3. Which are the principal parts of the Mass?
4. What are the words of consecration?
5. When was the first Mass said?
6. By what words did Jesus tell the Apostles that they should also say Mass?
7. On what days must a Catholic hear Mass?
8. What are the holydays of obligation and when are they celebrated?
9. What event is celebrated on each of these days?

Good things to read:

"Vestments," *Catholic Youth Reader V*, page 316.
"The Mass," *Shields Reader V*, page 212.
"An Exchange of Gifts," *American Reader V*, page 109.
"A Handboy of the Lord," *Catholic Youth Reader VI*, page 1.
"Sentence of Sir Thomas More," *Catholic National Reader VI*.
"Blessed Thomas More," *Heroes of God's Church*, Matimore, page 177.
"The Sacrifice of the Mass," *Marywood Reader V*, page 33.
"Getting Set," *Rosary Reader V*, page 53.
"The Altar Boy," *American Cardinal Reader V*, page 155.
"Blessed Thomas More," *Literature and Art IV*.

42. Daniel O'Connell

From the time of St. Patrick the faith of Ireland became so strong, and brought forth such heroic men and women, that the country was called the "Isle of Saints."

Great monasteries arose, out of which went holy missionaries to spread the faith in other countries.

In the twelfth century Ireland was conquered by England, and when later England herself turned Protestant under King Henry VIII, she did all in her power to tear Ireland away from the Church also. It was a terrible struggle, but Ireland as a whole never gave up the faith that St. Patrick had planted on its soil centuries before. Because the people clung to their faith, churches and convents were destroyed and all rights were taken away from them. To be a Catholic in Ireland from that time on, meant to be poor and persecuted, to be almost like a slave. Since, in spite of all their hardships, the Irish people would not give up their faith, the English did their best to make them die out slowly. This sad condition lasted for hundreds of years. From time to time the Irish people tried to regain some of their rights, but little could be done without a good leader.

Then in 1810 a fearless leader rose to carry on the fight for his enslaved people. That leader was Daniel O'Connell. He formed the Catholics into a strong party and by his fiery speeches brought courage back into their hearts. But no matter how bitter were their feelings toward England or how much they were wronged, he always kept them on the side of law and order. Through the efforts of the Catholic party, Daniel O'Connell was finally able to be their representative in the English Parliament, where he could fight better for their rights. In order to hold this office, however, he was expected to take an oath in which he had to deny important Catholic teachings. O'Connell refused to take the oath or to give up his office. Four million Irishmen were ready to stand by him. At last the king was forced to sign a bill which gave the Catholics of Ireland and all other countries under English rule, the right to practice their religion.

It was the beginning of a new life for Ireland. Yet, there was much still to be done. For eighteen years Daniel O'Connell fought to free his country from the rule of England. He did not succeed; but he had taught his countrymen how to stand up and fight for their Church and their country.

Daniel O'Connell was a lawyer. There are many interesting little stories told about his cleverness and ready wit in defending the right. One day he was defending a man by the name of James, who was accused of murder. A witness was up for examination and O'Connell felt that the man was not honest, although he had promised under oath to speak the truth. This witness swore that a hat which had been found near the murdered man belonged to James. O'Connell asked to see the hat. He looked carefully at the top, the rim, the whole outside. Then he examined the inside in the same way. All of a sudden he looked surprised. Turning the hat around slowly, he began to spell the word, "J–a–m–e–s." He turned to the witness.

"Now, do you mean to tell the court and the jury that this name was in the hat when you found it?"

"I do, on my oath," replied the witness.

"Did you see the name there?"

"I did, surely."

"This is the same hat? There is no mistake about it?"

"No mistake. It is the hat."

O'Connell turned in triumph to the judge.

"Your honor, there is an end to this case. There is no name in the hat."

To the last year of his life Daniel O'Connell fought and pleaded for his beloved country. There had been a great famine and he went to ask the help of England for the starving people in Ireland. "She is in your hands," he said, "in your power. If you do not save her, she cannot save herself."

Everybody listened to him with sympathy and respect, for he was now a sick and broken man. He had spent his strength in serving his Church and his country.

O'Connell had always wished to go to Rome, to the center of that faith for which he had spent his life. He started on his journey, but died in Genoa on May 15, 1847, without having reached Rome. His last request was: "Send my heart to Rome and my body to Ireland."

Now answer these questions:
   1. Why was Ireland called the "Isle of Saints"?
   2. Who conquered Ireland?
   3. What did England want the Irish people to do?
   4. What did it mean to be a Catholic in Ireland?
   5. Who became the fearless leader of the Irish in 1810?
   6. What did he do for them?

7. Why did O'Connell refuse to take the oath he was expected to take?

8. What right did the Catholics finally get?

9. Where did Daniel O'Connell die?

10. What was his last request?

* * *

With his last request Daniel O'Connell meant to say that his heart belonged to God and to his Church, while his bodily gifts were intended to serve his country. How well he knew how to use God's gifts.

Our country needs men and women who have the courage to stand by the right no matter what it costs. The boys and girls of today are the men and women of the future. They must learn to stand by the right while they are young. That is, they must form good habits that fit them for the best service they can give their country.

Make a list of good habits you must form to become of service to your country.

Look over the following quotations and see whether any of them will help you form better habits.

"My son, hear the instruction of thy father. And forsake not the law of thy mother." — *Bible.*

"Do unto others as you would have them do unto you."

"A wise man is always willing to learn."

"Lost time is never found again."

"A good name is better than a good face."

"Love your country, believe in her, honor her,
   Work for her, and live for her." — *Dufferin.*

"The secret of being lovely is being unselfish." — *J. G. Holland.*

"A willing helper does not wait till he is asked."

"Whoever you are, be noble;
  Whatever you do, do well;
 Whenever you speak, speak kindly,
  Give joy wherever you dwell." — *Ruskin.*

"No man is wise or safe, but he that is honest." — *Scott.*

Can you answer these questions?
  1. What is an oath?
  2. When may we take an oath?
  3. What commandment forbids us to lie?
  4. What else is forbidden by this commandment?

Good things to read:
 "Trust in God," *Ideal Reader V*, page 74.

43. Frederick Ozanam

We have heard much in late years about the Society of St. Vincent de Paul. It was founded in Paris by Frederick Ozanam, a young Frenchman, who called the society by the name of the great Apostle of Charity, St. Vincent de Paul.

Frederick Ozanam lived in Paris just a hundred years ago. At that time the minds of the French people had been poisoned by the teachings and writings of men who no longer believed in God. Especially in the universities the teachers were doing their best to spread unbelief and to kill the faith in the hearts of their pupils.

Frederick had been raised in the city of Lyons by

splendid Christian parents. But a time came in his young life when the teachings of unbelief caused him great temptations against his faith. He loved his faith and prayed with all his heart for the grace to remain true to the Church. God heard his prayers. The temptation

Frederick Ozanam.

passed away and Frederick was so grateful to God that he wished to spend his life in making the truth known to others.

Would God call him to the priesthood, he wondered, so that he might the better carry out this desire of his heart? He prayed and waited. And in His own good time, God showed him that his work was waiting for him at the University of Paris, where he had studied and where he was later to teach. He married a young woman whose piety and faith were as deep as his own. On the day of their wedding he told her how as a boy he had been tempted against the faith and how he had promised God to devote his life to the spread of the truth. Then he asked her to join him every day in thanking God for having kept him true to the Church. And from that time on to the end of his life, they made their act of thanksgiving together every day.

Already as a student of law he joined a group of Catholic young men to defend the faith. But it was as a teacher that his real work as an apostle began. His many pupils loved him and listened to his lectures with delight. For a teacher to defend his Catholic belief openly at the university in those days was to risk losing his position. But Ozanam never missed a chance to speak of religion when he felt that it would do good. One day a note was handed to him. It was written by one of his students and said among other things: "What a great number of sermons have failed to do for me, you have done in an hour: you have made me a Christian!" We can only guess what joy Frederick Ozanam felt when he read these words.

Because he defended the Catholic faith on all sides, he was attacked by many enemies of the Church. But, on the other hand, people admired his great learning, respected his piety, and loved him for his kindness. One thing the enemies often flung at the Catholics in those days: "You claim that the Catholic Church is not dead," they said. "Where are your works to prove it?" Ozanam began to think that something should be done to show that the Catholic faith was an active faith, that is, a faith that shows itself in good works. With a few friends he began to talk the matter over and finally they decided to form a little society for the help of the poor. That was the beginning of the Society of St. Vincent de Paul.

For a long time these few men, busy as they were, worked alone, visiting the sick and helping the poor. Then the good work spread, and before his death Ozanam and his companions had the joy of seeing 2,000 men join the society in Paris alone. In France there were 500 societies; and the good work spread also to England, Spain, Belgium, America, and even to Jerusalem.

Frederick Ozanam had worn himself out with work for others. When he was only 40 years old, a serious illness brought him to the end of his life. Before his death he had the happiness of visiting the Holy Father and the many holy places he had heard and read so much about and always longed to see.

He loved to read the Scriptures. During his last illness one could see him lying in his chair with the Bible open before him. In sickness as in health, a favorite act of Ozanam was to give thanks to God for all His goodness. Often he would count up the blessings he had received and ask his friends to join him in offering thanks to God.

After he had received the last sacraments, his brother

222221

spoke to him about God's mercy. "Why should I fear Him? I love Him so much!" said Ozanam.

He had spent his life in defending the Church and in doing works of mercy. He went to eternity with the sweet hope of a child meeting its beloved Father.

Now answer these questions:
1. What society did Frederick Ozanam found?
2. Where did he live?
3. How was Frederick Ozanam tempted?
4. Why was he grateful to God?
5. How did he wish to show his gratitude?
6. What did he tell his wife on the day of their wedding?
7. How did his pupils feel toward him?
8. Why did he think of forming a society to help the poor?
9. How many societies of St. Vincent de Paul were there in France before his death?
10. What did he say when he received the last sacraments?
11. What was his favorite act?

*   *   *

Frederick Ozanam loved to count the blessings he had received from God and to give thanks for them. We, too, have received many blessings from God. Do you ever stop to think about them? Do you thank God often for what He has given you?

See whether you can form the habit of counting your blessings as Ozanam did and giving thanks for them every day. Remember it takes much practice to form the habit.

Things to do:
1. Make a list of all the good things you have received from God.

2. Have you a Society of St. Vincent de Paul in your parish? If so, find out something about the work that the members do.

3. Plan something your class could do for the poor and tell your teacher about it.

4. What other persons have you read about who loved to read the Bible? Write their names.

5. Find a poem or prayer of thanks to God for all His gifts and read it to the class.

Can you answer these questions?

1. Who teaches us about God and all we must believe?
2. Is temptation a sin?
3. What should you do in temptation?
4. What is faith?
5. How does a person sin against faith?
6. May we ever deny our faith?
7. How do we fail to try to know what God has taught?
8. What are they called who do not believe what God has taught?

Good things to read:

"Henri Fabre," *Rosary Reader V*, page 297.

Test Yourself

A Game of Famous Sayings

Answer with the name of the person who spoke these words. Ten points is a perfect score.

1. My heart to Rome, my body to Ireland.
2. Lord Jesus, receive my spirit.
3. Our hearts are restless until they rest in Thee, O Lord.
4. Why should I fear Him? I love Him so much.

5. I would rather see you dead at my feet than have you commit a mortal sin.

6. I have fought a good fight, I have finished my course, I have kept the faith.

7. Trifles make perfection, but perfection is no trifle.

8. I desire nothing but Thee, O Lord.

9. You can catch more flies with a spoonful of honey than with a barrel of vinegar.

10. All things pass away.

UNIT XIV

The Church and Peace

More than seven hundred years before Christ came to earth, the prophet Isaias said of Him:

"And His name shall be called Wonderful,
Counsellor,
God the Mighty,
The Father of the World to Come,
The Prince of Peace."

And when the angels appeared to the shepherds on Christmas night to announce His coming, they sang: "Glory to God in the highest and on earth peace to men of good will." Wherever Christ went during His life on earth, He brought peace. The Apostles carried the message of the Prince of Peace to distant countries, and their successors, the popes and bishops, have done everything in their power since to bring peace to the world.

Before our own Holy Father, Pius XI became the head of the Church, Benedict XV ruled as pope. He was called the "Pope of Peace" by a world which was engaged in a bitter and fearful war. In the next lesson we shall see how this pope came to earn such a wonderful title.

44. Peace Be With You

On the highest point of a pass in the Andes Mountains, on the border line between Argentina and Chile, stands a large statue of Christ. His right hand is raised upward, while His left holds a large cross. The following words are written on the base on which the statue rests: "Peace to all nations. Sooner shall these mountains crumble into dust than Argentina and Chile break the peace they have pledged at the feet of Christ, their Savior."

When these two countries made peace with each other, they remembered that all Christian people are brothers in Christ, and that God is their Father. With these thoughts in mind, they could not have hatred in their hearts. Christ, they knew, loved them all; Christ died for all; Christ forgave them their sins. They were children of the same Father, branches of the same Vine. And therefore they made an everlasting peace, and in memory of their promise, erected the beautiful statue of Christ, high up in the mountains, where He looks down upon the people of both nations as if to say: "Peace I leave you, My peace I give to you."

In spite of the fact that the Church has always preached peace, we know that there have been many wars in the history of the world. One of the greatest and most terrible was the World War which started in 1914. Most of the great nations of the world took part in this awful struggle. More than ever, men forgot the teachings of the Prince of Peace. It looked for a time as if the whole world would continue to fight until nothing but ruins remained.

Then, in the same year that the World War began, Pope Pius X died, and Pope Benedict XV was elected to take his place. What would and what could the new pope do to bring back peace? All around him were hatred and bloodshed, suffering and starvation. He had no troops, he had no temporal power. He was an Italian, and Italy had also entered the World War.

Benedict XV understood his duty as head of the Church. He was the father of all Christians. He belonged not to Italy but to the whole world. His heart went out to his suffering children in every country of the world, whether they fought with or against Italy. But what could he do to help them? Three times at the beginning of the war, he wrote to the rulers of the different nations, begging them to put an end to the awful struggle. When he heard of the unfair treatment of one nation by another, he fearlessly protested against the wrong before the whole world.

Nor did the Holy Father stop at words. He gave money freely for the relief of the war victims, for the wounded, the widows, the orphans. He made a plan by means of which the prisoners of war could write to their families. And all the time he was being closely watched by those who hate the Church and the pope, to see whether he could not be caught doing something with which they could find fault. But even the bitterest enemies of the pope had to admit that he remained strictly neutral and that he was doing all in his power to bring peace to the world.

When the war was ended at last, the heart of Benedict XV was glad. But he knew that although the treaty of peace was signed, peace had not yet come into the hearts of men. Hatred, poverty, misery, and famine could not be stopped by a treaty. Justice and charity had to take the place of hatred and revenge if all this terrible suffering was to end. And so the pope wrote an encyclical on peace, which helped more than anything else to bring the nations more closely together again. In this encyclical, the pope reminded the nations of the great law of love which Christ had given to all people. "The Gospel," he says in his letter, "does not contain one law of charity for individuals and another law, different from the first, for cities and nations." He also says that treaties of peace will be of no help unless the nations practice charity toward one another and put all hatred out of their hearts.

Proudly the children of the Church looked up to Pope Benedict as a true follower of Him who had come to bring peace to men of good will, and proudly they have given him the title "Pope of Peace."

Again the Church had shown, as she had so often in the past, that she is the mother of all children and more especially the mother of the weak and the oppressed Glorious Church of Christ, founded by the Prince of Peace!

Now answer these questions:

1. What words are written under the statue of Christ?
2. Why did Argentina and Chile make peace?
3. Which was one of the greatest wars ever fought?
4. Who was elected pope at that time?
5. To what country did the pope belong?
6. Did he side with Italy?
7. What are some of the things the Holy Father did during the war?
8. What did the pope say about treaties of peace?
9. What title was given to Pope Benedict XV?

* * *

It is a wonderful thing to be at peace with everyone; with God, with our neighbor, and with ourselves.

We are at peace with God if we love Him above all things and keep our hearts free from sin so that He can enter in.

We are at peace with our neighbor when we practice the great commandment: "Thou shalt love thy neighbor as thyself."

We are at peace with ourselves if we trust in God and believe that whatever happens to us is just as He wills it and because He wills it.

Ask yourself:

Am I at peace with everyone?

Do I keep my heart free from sin?

If I have committed a mortal sin, do I go to confession as soon as possible?

Do I make an act of contrition every night?

Do I hate anyone?

Am I willing to forgive if anyone has hurt me?

Am I kind to my neighbor?

Am I just to my neighbor?

Do I remember that people of other countries are also my neighbors?

Am I quarrelsome?

Do I always keep the best for myself or do I share what I have with others?

Do I remember that God knows best what is good for me?

Things to do:

1. See whether you can find a picture of the Christ of the Andes and something about the story.

2. Locate the Andes Mountains, Argentina, and Chile on the map.

3. Sometimes our Lord is pictured as the Prince of Peace. See whether you can find a picture by that title.

4. Pope Benedict died in 1922. How long did he reign? When did the World War end and how long did it last?

5. Find the Beatitude that speaks about peacemakers.

6. Nearly every day at Mass the priest says a prayer for peace. In your prayer book or missal find the prayer. It follows the *Agnus Dei*. Memorize the prayer and say it often.

7. In this book find the story of another great pope that helped to make peace between princes and nations. Also find a woman saint who worked for peace between the pope and the nations.

Can you answer these questions?

1. How did Jesus show that He loved all men?

2. Why did Jesus die for us?

3. Do you think it is always wrong to have war?

4. Against what commandment is hatred? quarreling?

5. Who is the Prince of Peace?

6. Why is He called the Prince of Peace?

7. When did the Prince of Peace come to earth?

8. How can we be at peace with God? with our neighbor? with ourselves?

Good things to read:

"A Story of the World War," *American Reader V*, page 346.

"The Little Flags," *Cathedral Basic Reader V*, page 423.

"Friendship Among Nations," *Rosary Reader IV*, page 231.

"World Peace," *Rosary Reader IV*, page 206.

GLORIA IN EXCELSIS DEO

Gloria in excelsis Deo,

Et in terra pax hominibus bonae voluntatis.

Laudamus te.

Benedicimus te.

Adoramus te.

Glorificamus te.

Gratias agimus tibi propter magnam gloriam tuam.

Domine Deus, Rex coelestis,

Deus Pater omnipotens.

Domine, Fili unigenite, Jesu Christe.

Domine Deus, Agnus Dei, Filius Patris.

Qui tollis peccata mundi,

Miserere nobis.

Qui tollis peccata mundi,

GLORY TO GOD IN THE HIGHEST

Glory to God in the highest,

And on earth peace to men of good will.

We praise Thee,

We bless Thee,

We adore Thee,

We glorify Thee.

We give Thee thanks for Thy great glory.

O Lord God, heavenly King,

God the Father almighty.

O Lord Jesus Christ, the only-begotten Son.

O Lord God, Lamb of God, Son of the Father.

Who takest away the sins of the world,

Have mercy upon us.

Who takest away the sins of the world,

Suscipe deprecationem nostram.

Receive our prayer.

Qui sedes ad dexteram patris,

Who sittest at the right hand of the Father,

Miserere nobis.

Have mercy upon us.

Quoniam tu solus Sanctus.

For Thou only art holy.

Tu solus Dominus.

Thou only art Lord.

Tu solus Altissimus, Jesu Christe.

Thou only, O Jesus Christ, Art most high,

Cum Sancto Spiritu,

Together with the Holy Ghost,

In gloria Dei Patris. Amen.

In the glory of God the Father. Amen.

UNIT XV

You Are the Branches

Jesus once said, "Without Me you can do nothing." We know how true that is. We are the branches of the true Vine and a branch cannot live by itself. Its life and its strength come from the Vine. Whenever we see a branch with fresh green leaves and beautiful fruit, we know that it is a living, healthy branch, which is closely united with the other branches and especially with the stem that holds them all together. Whenever a branch is torn loose from the vine, it withers and dies.

"I am the Vine, you are the branches." Through all the years, since those words were spoken by Christ, the branches, the children of the Church, have spread out and borne fruit. Today we are those branches. Our life and our strength come from the Vine, but the fruit we must bring forth also ourselves. We must be not only Catholics, we must be living, active Catholics. We must not only love our faith, we must show that we love it, we must live it. Then shall we gather more and more strength from the Vine and bear glorious fruit.

Once more we shall look back over the history of the Church and then go in person to the Holy Father to tell him that we wish always to remain faithful branches of the true Vine.

45. The Church Still Lives

Today we are going to make a long, long journey. We are going back over the ages, 1900 years, and follow the Church from its beginning to the present day.

Beginning with the first Pentecost Day, the Apostles went out to different countries to teach all nations, as Christ had commanded them. They were received with joy by some, with bitter hatred by others. All but one of the Apostles were put to death, but the Church continued to live.

Then came the pagan Roman emperors and said: "The Christians must be wiped from the face of the earth. Not one must be left to tell the story of Christ. Search for them in all the corners of the empire. Torture them, throw them to the wild beasts, burn them, behead them." The bloody work went on for three hundred years. Christians were martyred by the thousands, yes, by the hundreds of thousands. Finally the victory of Constantine brought freedom to the Church. The Christians crept out of the catacombs and other hiding places. They built churches and converted the pagans on all sides. A new and happy life began for the Christians. Every day the Church became greater and stronger. The cruel persecutors were dead, but the Church still lived.

But soon another storm arose. Swarms of barbarians swept over Europe and tore down everything in their way. They burned churches and homes, dragged their victims with them or left them dead upon the ground. When they had finished their work of destruction, the Roman Empire was in ruins. Nothing was left of civilization in the western world; nothing but the Church. And she set out at once to begin her work anew.

Making Christians out of these barbarian tribes was not the work of a few years, but of hundreds of years. The missionaries had to teach them not only to know the true God but also to cultivate the soil and to live peacefully among themselves. By and by the new nations became Christian. Emperors like Charlemagne helped the Church in her work of spreading the faith, and the Church helped the emperors by making their subjects better citizens and holier men.

In the Middle Ages the deep and beautiful faith of the people showed itself in all they did. They raised great cathedrals to the glory of God, who meant more to them than anything else. They honored God and His Blessed Mother by paintings which are more beautiful than any that an artist can make today. They brought forth religious statues and writings that cannot be imitated. They set out on the Crusades and fought for the Holy Land, where Christ had lived and died. It was an age of glorious faith, a faith which all the people lived and loved. No wonder it showed itself so beautifully in all their works.

Up to this time all the countries of Europe were happily united in the one Christian faith. The pope was the spiritual father to whom all nations looked as their leader. But sad days were ahead. Soon there was trouble in the Church itself. False teachings were spread, first in Germany and then in many other European countries. Whole nations separated themselves from the true Vine. Hatred, persecution, and bloody wars followed. It was a terrible Revolution, started by Martin Luther and continued by other rebellious children of the Church. Those who did not remember the words of Christ said that the Church had come to an end at last. And her enemies were glad. But in the meantime great armies of saintly men went out to bring the lost sheep back to the fold. The Council of Trent, like a skillful doctor, cut away what was bad or dead and bound up the wounds that had been made by the enemy. Slowly but surely the Church arose once more, strong and beautiful as ever.

Since that time the enemies of the Church have tried harder than ever to crush her. In some countries rulers were so blind as to believe that they could tear the faith out of the hearts of men. They have closed churches and forbidden people to worship God. They have done their wicked deeds and then died. And the Church still lives.

If you look around today, you will find that the Church still has her enemies. But she stands quiet and unafraid. She has lived through the ages, she will con-

The Corpus Christi Procession in Rome, June, 1934.

tinue to live to the end of time. The gates of hell shall not prevail against her.

And we, who are children of that glorious Church, how proud we should be to belong to her. Shall we allow the enemy to tear us away? No, never! We belong to Christ and His Church. As long as we remain with Him, we shall live and bring forth fruit. He is the Vine, we are the branches. And as a pledge of our loyalty to His Church, we shall now rise and repeat with the many martyrs and saints and children of the Church through all the ages,

"I believe in God, the Father Almighty, Creator of heaven and earth. And in Jesus Christ, His only Son, our Lord: Who was conceived by the Holy Ghost, born of the Virgin Mary, suffered under Pontius Pilate, was crucified, died, and was buried. He descended into hell, the third day He arose again from the dead. He ascended into heaven, sitteth at the right hand of God the Father Almighty. From thence He shall come to judge the living and the dead. I believe in the Holy Ghost, the holy Catholic Church, the communion of saints, the forgiveness of sins, the resurrection of the body, and life everlasting. Amen."

46. Roma!

All aboard for Rome! The train is waiting and we must hurry. We wave good-by to our friends and off we

300 THE VINE AND THE BRANCHES

speed to New York. There we board a steamer and settle down for the journey across the Atlantic.

At last we are going to Rome! As we sit back in our comfortable steamer chairs and watch the waves rise and fall, our thoughts are already in the Eternal City.

Once upon a time the princes of the Apostles walked along the roads that we shall soon walk. Nero feasted in his garden there, while the Christians served as living torches. There the great Apostles Peter and Paul preached the faith and gave up their lives. In the Roman circus, which still stands, Christians were torn by lions and tigers and bulls. We imagine ourselves walking through the Arch of Constantine, the same through which he marched with his victorious army in the year 312. We shall go down deep into the catacombs, the burial places of the early martyrs.

Of course we shall visit the oldest of all churches, the Lateran, and see the great St. Peter's, the largest and most wonderful church in all the world. Then there will be the statue of Moses to look at, that great masterpiece of Michelangelo's, and many of the paintings done by the hand of Raphael.

For nearly two weeks we are on the way. And then, one glorious morning, we are awakened by the cry, "Roma!" Our hearts are thrilled, our eyes overflow with tears of joy. We are in the Eternal City.

We make our way over the Tiber bridge, straight to St. Peter's. Near the great dome is the Vatican palace, the home of the Holy Father. Passing the Swiss Guard, we go up the marble stairs and along the long hallways, until we reach the audience chamber, the place where we shall see the Holy Father. Thousands of people are already assembled there, people of all countries and all

Our Holy Father, Pope Pius XI.

races. We take our places among them and wait. Suddenly everything becomes very quiet. We hold our breath. The high folding doors open and — the Holy Father enters.

"Thou art Peter, and on this rock I will build My Church," we say to ourselves, trembling with joy.

Different people are being presented to him now. At last comes our turn.

"Holy Father," we say, "we are your children from America. For the last year we have been learning about the history of the Church. We have come to tell you that we are proud to belong to that great Church and that we shall always be her faithful and obedient children."

The Holy Father answers: "My dear children, little lambs of the fold of Christ, I pray that the good Shepherd may always keep you near Him." And as he raises his hand in blessing, we fall on our knees and bow our heads.

The next moment all is over. We hardly know where we are going. There are many things we hear and see after that, but one thing alone stands out in our memory. It is our visit to the Holy Father.

Things to do:

1. Learn what you can about Vatican City in Rome, which belongs to the pope, and tell the class something interesting you have read.

2. Find a picture of St. Peter's dome and put it on the bulletin board.

3. Show a picture of the Roman circus and tell about some martyr who died there.

4. Pretend you were down in the catacombs and tell in a letter to a friend how you felt and what you saw.

5. Trace the route from your home to Rome.

6. If you know a priest or someone else who has been in Rome, invite him to tell your class about his visit.

7. Find a picture of the Arch of Constantine and tell the story of the victory of Constantine.

8. Find out what you can about the Swiss Guard and how they are dressed.

9. Give a little talk to the class about St. Peter's or the Lateran Church.

10. Draw one or more of the symbols of faith that are carved on the stones in the catacombs.

Good things to read:

"Saint John Lateran," *Rosary Reader IV*, page 296.

"Our Titles," *Shields Reader V*, page 199.

"St. Peter's Church at Rome," *Shields Reader V*, page 231.

"Vicar of Christ," *American Reader V*, page 20.

"The Hour of Prayer," *Ideal Reader V*, page 267.

"The Church of Rome," *Shields Reader V*, page 215.

Now answer these questions:

1. How many were converted when St. Peter gave his first sermon on Pentecost Day?

2. What is meant by the Church?

3. Who belong to the Church?

4. Who is the visible and who is the invisible head of the Church?

5. How and where were SS. Peter and Paul put to death?

6. How were the Christians treated in Rome?

7. Who gave freedom to the early Church and why?

8. How was the Roman Empire destroyed?

9. Find the names of two great missionaries who left their own country to convert the pagans of other lands.

10. Under what great Christian ruler did the Church and the emperor work together for the good of both?

11. How did the deep faith of the people in the Middle Ages show itself?

12. What words of Christ did they not remember who thought the Church had come to an end?

13. Who were the great armies of men that went to bring the sheep back to the fold?

14. Do you know of any countries that have tried to put the Church out of their land altogether?

15. What enemies has the Church today?

16. How can we be torn from the Church?

17. What must we do to remain good Catholics?

18. What must we be careful not to do?

19. What does the Apostles' Creed contain?

20. What Creed is said or sung at Mass?

A GAME WITH THE SAINTS

What saint is represented with

1. Keys
2. Shamrock
3. A child on his shoulder
4. Roses dropping down to earth
5. A lamb
6. A lily and a skull
7. An eagle
8. A dragon at the horse's feet
9. An infant wrapped in his cloak
10. A cross in the shape of an X

Who is the special patron of

1. Doctors
2. Artists
3. All charity societies
4. Negroes
5. Foreign missions
6. Farmers
7. Carpenters
8. Hunters
9. Motorists
10. Musicians
11. Stone masons
12. Nurses
13. Cooks and housewives
14. Singers
15. Dentists

Who is the special patron of
1. Germany
2. Ireland
3. England
4. Scotland
5. Paris

6. Venice
7. France
8. United States
9. Spain
10. India

What feast is celebrated on each of the following days:
1. October 3
2. April 23
3. January 25
4. January 29
5. May 3
6. January 6
7. December 8
8. March 7

9. December 26
10. February 11
11. July 26
12. September 8
13. June 24
14. October 15
15. October 2

PRAYERS

The Sign of the Cross
In the name of the Father, and of the Son, and of the Holy Ghost. Amen.

The Our Father
Our Father, Who art in heaven, hallowed be Thy name. Thy kingdom come, Thy will be done on earth as it is in heaven.

Give us this day our daily bread, and forgive us our trespasses as we forgive those who trespass against us. And lead us not into temptation, but deliver us from evil. Amen.

The Hail Mary
Hail, Mary, full of grace, the Lord is with thee. Blessed art thou among women, and blessed is the fruit of thy womb, Jesus.

Holy Mary, Mother of God, pray for us sinners, now and at the hour of our death. Amen.

The Apostles' Creed
I believe in God, the Father Almighty, Creator of heaven and earth. And in Jesus Christ, His only Son, our Lord: Who was conceived by the Holy Ghost, born of the Virgin Mary, suffered under Pontius Pilate, was crucified, died, and was buried. He descended into Hell, the third day He arose from the dead. He ascended into Heaven, sitteth at the right hand of God the Father Almighty. From thence He shall come to judge the living and the dead. I believe in the Holy Ghost, the Holy Catholic Church, the communion of saints, the forgiveness of sins, the resurrection of the body, and life everlasting. Amen.

An Act of Faith
O my God! I firmly believe that Thou art one God in three Divine Persons, Father, Son, and Holy Ghost. I believe that the Divine Son became man, and died for our sins, and that He will come to judge the living and the dead. I believe these and all the truths which the Holy Catholic Church teaches, because Thou hast revealed them, Who canst neither deceive nor be deceived.

An Act of Hope

O my God! Relying on Thy infinite goodness and promises, I hope to obtain pardon of my sins, the help of Thy Grace, and life everlasting, through the merits of Jesus Christ, my Lord and Redeemer.

An Act of Charity, or Love

O my God! I love Thee above all things, with my whole heart and soul, because Thou art all-good and worthy of all love. I love my neighbor as myself, for love of Thee. I forgive all who have injured me, and ask pardon of all whom I have injured.

An Act of Contrition

O my God! I am heartily sorry for having offended Thee, and I detest all my sins, because I dread the loss of heaven and the pains of hell, but most of all because they offend Thee, my God, Who art all-good and deserving of all my love. I firmly resolve, with the help of Thy grace, to confess my sins, to do penance, and to amend my life.

The Confiteor, or I Confess

I confess to Almighty God, to blessed Mary ever Virgin, to blessed Michael the Archangel, to blessed John the Baptist, to the holy Apostles Peter and Paul, and to all the saints, that I have sinned exceedingly in thought, word, and deed, *through my fault, through my fault, through my most grievous fault.* Therefore, I beseech blessed Mary ever Virgin, blessed Michael the Archangel, blessed John the Baptist, the holy Apostles Peter and Paul, and all the saints, to pray to the Lord our God for me.

May the Almighty God have mercy on me, forgive me my sins, and bring me to everlasting life. Amen.

May the Almighty and Merciful Lord grant me pardon, absolution, and remission of all my sins. Amen.

The Gloria Patri, or the Lesser Doxology

Glory be to the Father, and to the Son, and to the Holy Ghost. As it was in the beginning, is now, and ever shall be, world without end. Amen.

Prayer to the Guardian Angel

Angel of God, my guardian dear,
To whom His love commits me here,
Ever this day be at my side
To light, to guard, to rule and guide.
Amen.

The Angelus

(At morning, noon, and night)

V. The angel of the Lord declared unto Mary.

R. And she conceived of the Holy Ghost.

Hail Mary, etc.

V. Behold the handmaid of the Lord.

R. Be it done unto me according to Thy word.

Hail Mary, etc.

V. And the Word was made flesh.

R. And dwelt among us.

Hail Mary, etc.

V. Pray for us, O holy Mother of God.

R. That we may be made worthy of the promises of Christ.

Blessing Before Meals

Bless us, O Lord, and these Thy gifts, which we are about to receive from Thy bounty, through Christ our Lord. Amen.

Thanksgiving After Meals

We return Thee thanks, Almighty God, for these Thy benefits, which we have received from Thy bounty, through Christ, our Lord. Amen.

Prayer Before a Crucifix

A plenary indulgence may be gained after Confession and Holy Communion by *saying* this prayer before a crucifix or a picture of one. Granted by Pope Pius IX, July 31, 1858.

Behold, O kind and most sweet Jesus, I cast myself on my knees in Thy sight, and with the most fervent desire of my soul I pray and beseech Thee to fix deep in my soul lively sentiments of faith, hope, and charity, with true repentance for my sins, and a firm desire of amendment, while with deep love and grief of soul I ponder within myself and mentally contemplate Thy five most precious wounds; having before my eyes that which David spoke in prophecy: "They have pierced My Hands and My Feet; they have numbered all My Bones."

Say some prayers for the intention of the Holy Father.

CPSIA information can be obtained
at www.ICGtesting.com
Printed in the USA
FSHW012112181119
64225FS